OMAR WEDDERBURN

LIVING ON THE *Edge* OF A BREAKTHROUGH

OMAR WEDERBURN

DAYELight PUBLISHERS

LIVING ON THE EDGE OF A BREAKTHROUGH
Copyright © 2018
by Bishop O'mar Wedderburn.
All rights reserved; printed in the United States of America. Except for brief quotations in critical articles or reviews, no part of this book may be used or reproduced in any manner whatsoever without written permission.

All scriptures are taken from the Holy Bible, New King James Version Copyright

© 1982 by Thomas Nelson, Inc. Used by permission. All rights reserved. The Bible used was the Holy Bible NKJV, Nashville: Thomas Nelson, 1994.

Scripture quotations marked as KJV are from the HOLY BIBLE, KING JAMES VERSION, © 1972, 1976, 1979, 1983, 1984, 1985 Thomas Nelson Inc.

Scripture quotations noted NASB are from the New American Standard Bible ®, © Copyright The Lockman Foundation 1960, 1963, 1963, 1968,

1971, 1972, 1973, 1975, 1977. All rights reserved. Used by permission.

Scripture quotations marked "NIV" are taken from HOLY BIBLE, NEW INTERNATIONAL VERSION. Copyright 1973, 1978, 1984 by International Bible Society. Used by permission of Zondervan Publishing House.

ISBN: 978-0-9994025-9-7 (Paperback)

OMAR WEDDERBURN

DEDICATION

I dedicate this book to Mrs. Pauline Blake-Miller. All that I have become is primarily due to you, mother. Your life exemplifies pure kindness, sincerity, and a lovable soul – traits I have inherited and promise to pass on to my children. Writing this book, I encountered many challenges, but you never raised me to be a quitter, and the values you instilled within me gave me the drive to overcome these challenges. Mother, take a bow; you have done exceptionally well. You are precious, and I love you dearly. Thank You, Lord, for allowing her to carry me for nine months.

I also dedicate this book to my son, Christian, my little "Bear." As your grandmother raised and taught me to be a gentleman, I relay this instruction to you, son. You were given the name "follower of Christ" for a purpose, and it is my constant prayer that you become the mighty man of God you are destined to be. It is every good father's legacy for their children to be more excellent than they were. Christian, it is your destiny to be greater and continue the thriving legacy handed down from your grandmother. I see every bit of me in you and am incredibly proud of you. Thank you for being a great son.

ACKNOWLEDGMENTS

Foremost, I thank my heavenly Father for giving me the strength, revelation, and inspiration to make this book a reality. Writing this book was not my doing but His. Thank you, Daddy, for considering me worthy of your gift and calling.

Thanks to my wonderful family. Your dedication, support, prayers, and encouragement are overwhelming and greatly appreciated. My siblings, Sasha and Larouux, thank you for motivating me to write. You two believed in me more than I did for myself.

Crystal S. Daye, my publisher, thank you dearly for believing in me. Your tremendous support and patience are greatly appreciated. This book is your doing as much as it is mine.

Thanks to Stephanie Prince, Tasharae Nicholson, and Deadranne Boston-Morrison. We deeply cherish your assistance in making this a reality.

Thanks to my spiritual sisters, Yasheka Sewell and Aphia Brown, for your financial support. I pray as you have sowed into this work, the Lord will sow into your lives bountifully.

Dr. Letitia McPherson, my spiritual mother, thank you for your continuous phone calls and check-ins. You saw me as greater than who I am and have always been passionate about bringing out the best in me. I recall your words, "Go ahead, man of God", when I told you my intention to write a book. You have always been supportive.

My Kingdom brothers and sisters, thank you for being a part of my life. You are the best!

Thank you, Carone Messado, my assistant pastor: my church family, Mofari. You guys are such a wonderful group. Love you to the core.

To all detractors and naysayers, I thank you for your opposition. It was the motivation I needed to complete the task. Strangely, your negativities and hatred were inadvertent strengths and revelations received in my completing this book.

Lastly, thank you to Terry-Ann Wedderburn. Every word in this book would not have been possible without your... You were a primary force and inspiration in more ways than one.

TABLE OF CONTENTS

Dedication III
Acknowledgments IV
Introduction VII
Chapter 1: Matter Of Time 1
Chapter 2: Walking In God's Promises 11
Chapter 3: It Will Be Ok 22
Chapter 4: I Am Purposed 30
Chapter 5: Help 46
Chapter 6: Possessing A Winning Mindset 54
Chapter 7: Against All Odds (You Can Still Win) 61
Chapter 8: "A Desperate Tear" 78
Chapter 9: I Will Not Be Wearied 86
Chapter 10: Living On The Edge 91
Chapter 11: Then Suddenly 99
Chapter 12: There Is A Cause 105
Wisdom Nuggets And Expressions 116
Scriptures For Consideration 125
About Author 127
Other Books By The Author 129

OMAR WEDDERBURN

INTRODUCTION

Some years ago, I started a project I thought to be divinely inspired and was eager to see it through. However, along the way, I failed miserably. I was discouraged and blamed God for my failure rather than accepting the demise as my own. Many Christians are guilty of this - prompted to blame the Lord, everyone, and everything for their shortcomings rather than themselves. The believers should not be surprised at disappointment, knowing that life will pitch a few curve balls. However, not all shortcomings end in failures but are propellers to a higher level of awareness. Hence, disappointment should not be a benchmark for quitting; worse than disappointment is not learning anything from it. The unwillingness to quit is critical to gaining success

I recall a portrait I had seen some years ago of a man digging for gold in what appears to be a cave. He was digging for a long time without any success. Frustrated, he walks away, but unbeknown to him, he is just some inches away from mining the valuable metal, based on the sketch's illustration. How familiar is this picture of your life? You put in your time, heart, and energy, but they seemed wasted, so you gave up and walked away - unknown to how close you were to triumph.

Failure can drive people to the point of quitting as they feel all hope is lost. Many failures are consequences of uncalculated and premature decisions - if they had counted and considered the essentials of accomplishing an aim, they would not have deserted the process. It would surprise many if they found out how close they were to the breakthrough. Therefore, one's drive should not be only to attain the goal but, more importantly, to endure the process that leads to the goal.

I believe the Lord allows the committed ones to be in hostile situations to demonstrate His faithfulness and empowers them to dominate. Let me explain by using Daniel as a figurative example - the Lord allowed him to be put in the lions' den, but then he turned around and made it his den - instead of the lions consuming Daniel, the Lord gave him dominion over the lions. So, cease with your complaint about being cast to lions and seize authority in owning the den.

Some Christians do find this saying disturbing - as they would rather not be placed with the lions – seeking an easy way out. If the majority of clergy were teaching patience and endurance during hardship, which is what this book is about, there would be significant changes in the mindset of believers - they would appreciate suffering (for the sake of Christ) as a privilege, not punishment. With this mindset, they will be confident that they are not suffering as an evildoer or a busybody in other men's matters. They will 'let patience have her perfect work, that they may be perfect and entirely wanting nothing.' (1 Peter 4:15, James 1:4)

The overwhelming popularity of the "prosperity gospel" is responsible for the deception that suffering is a result of a lack of faith. Its misconceptions have brainwashed many and must be corrected. I am appalled that those adherents of this faulty teaching believe it's a lie. Have they forgotten that longsuffering is a fruit of the Spirit?

This book helps expose the misconception and allows readers to know the valid message and power of longsuffering - the believers are partakers of Christ's suffering, and when they do, they shall reign with Him. So, the absolute truth is there is no prosperity without longsuffering - an opportunity will not fall from the sky because a believer "named it and claimed it." Wise up! Prosperity cohorts are only teaching one-half of the truth.

On the aforementioned note, this book is also geared toward highlighting the realities of the Christian's journey (not just the strengths but also the strains). It depicts the Christians' drive and their frustrations on faith's journey.

I aim to inspire readers to overcome inevitable discomforts on the path of righteousness, to be resolute, and to utilize sufferings (which God allows to build faith and relationship with the believers) as stepping stones to excellence.

LIVING ON THE EDGE OF A BREAKTHROUGH

Chapter 1
Matter Of Time

"For I know the plans I have for you," declares the LORD, "plans to prosper you and not to harm you, plans to give you hope and a future. Jeremiah 29:11

How many times have you been given a word that does not correspond with your current situation? What do you do when both are seemingly on a path of collision? Do you continue to believe or conclude that the word given was a lie? The truth is everyone, at some point, must come to grips with the reality of a failed expectation. Can you recall how often your expectations conflicted with reality and how difficult it was for you to choose?

This can be compared to Sarah's response to the Lord when told she would conceive a child, though barren and of old age. How would you handle this word if you were in her position? Would you find it preposterous and laugh as Sarah did? We have sometimes questioned our faith – not in the capacity of disbelief but in decision-making - you partly believe the word while questioning your decision. Such conflict thwarts sound judgment. If your primary focus is your experience (what is seen and felt), you will only second-guess your move forward. Thus, thoughts like, 'Should I continue to rely on God and His word or quit while I have the chance?' become normal responses, leading to a crossroads. However, if your focus is to stay the course - having eyes fixed on the expected prize, you will ignore the distractions and trust the Lord to keep His commitment according to His word.

Some people see themselves as worthless and unnoticed. They come to this conclusion based on a perception that their lives are meaningless compared to others. For people like this to succeed, they must first rid themselves of the delusion that everything that glitters is gold. Secondly, they must stop absorbing self-defeating thoughts - calm down, embrace positivity, and put everything in perspective. One's environment can indeed shape thinking and behaviour. However, the faithful believers' conviction is anchored in God's promises - it is driven by divine providence, not coincidence.

So, be comforted in the Lord's promises, knowing you are unique in His eyes. Remain faithful when being ignored - He will elevate you before others for your loyalty.

YOU ARE NOT AN AFTERTHOUGHT

According to John 1:1, the Word is God. The Word (logos) is the expressed thought of God. He and His Word are inseparable. When God created Adam, He designed him in His image. However, God's image of Adam was not limited to a body formed from malleable material (clay/dust of the ground). I suggest Adam was a thought of God way before he was formed in the likeness of God.

In other words, God had an image-nation of Adam before He formed an actual image of Adam - he was the result of God's thought/imagination brought to life. This concludes that Adam was not an afterthought and, subsequently, mankind. So, since mankind is not an afterthought, we must conclude that neither is mankind's redemption. Especially when it is taken into account that Jesus was slain before the foundations of the Earth. Hence, since salvation came through Jesus' work at the cross, done before the earth's foundations, grace is not an afterthought. Therefore, the believers should take comfort in this fact - their victory is imminent. On this premise, the body of Christ builds its faith and holds its trust in the word of God.

DELAY MEANS IT IS NOT YET TIME

"For the vision is yet for an appointed time, but at the end, it shall speak, and not lie though it tarry, wait for it; because it will surely come, it will not tarry" (Habakkuk 2:3).

Joseph had firsthand experience of the verse as mentioned earlier. His vision took thirteen years to come to pass. Every one of those days was miserable for Joseph, and perhaps, like many Christians, he questioned the validity of the vision. Yet, he remained faithful to the end. Delayed hope is not a failed hope. In my twenty-five years of ministry, I have come to appreciate delays. Why? Because I have become fully aware that delays, particularly the ones related to faithful believers, mean one thing – it is not time yet. Unfortunately, too many Christians refuse to wait on God's timing and abort the process. I have learned over the years that faith that has not been tested cannot be trusted. Interestingly, anything tested has been proven, tried, counted worthy, and approved. Approval is highly dependent on processing, which can be cumbersome for the individual who must endure, but the procedure will be credible. This is like

Peter's analogy (1 Peter 7) of gold that must pass through fire to be purified.

Note that the gold did not change until it had gone through the process of fire and was proven pure. Likewise, God allows believers to experience delayed expectations so that we can be fully processed and, in time, approved for the task. David is a perfect example. Samuel anointed him to be the next king of Israel, yet immediately after he had been anointed, he went back to caring for his father's sheep. Why? Because it was not his time to ascend to the throne. He had to go through the process, which took him over thirteen years. His expectation was delayed, but it was never denied. Ultimately, the believers' expectations must be built on the promises of God. When He gives a promise, He has no desire to break it. Therefore, remain faithful even during a holdup.

BEING LAST DOESN'T MEAN YOU ARE LEAST

Adam was the last thing God created, according to the creation account of Genesis. However, though Adam was last, he was on God's mind first - all He created before Adam He created for Adam. Thus, the reason why God had not created Adam first - until He had made a place for him. Adam was put on hold. However, whilst Adam was the last thing created, he was in no wise the least. Everything Adam inherited; he had dominion over them - his position did not affect his possession - his being on hold did not mean there was no connection. So, take comfort and quit complaining about you being worthless.

If you think God has forgotten and forsaken you because of a seeming silence, be assured your faithfulness has not gone unnoticed. See the holding period as His preparation for what awaits you. It is just a matter of time.

ORDER IS THE ORDER OF THE DAY

Time requires patience, and patience requires forbearance (of which, when all three are interwoven, produces order). Where there is no order, chaos is imminent. Those unwilling to exercise patience have no tolerance and, most times, will end up in chaos.

An example of order is a group of people correctly queued and organized outside a venue waiting to enter. But if everyone ignores the rules and tries to enter simultaneously, this will create mayhem. On this note, I desire you to see faithfulness as an organized queue and disobedience as an unruly mob. Regardless of how far back in the queue you feel, don't try to break the line. Be patient, endure, and persevere, as it is only a matter of time until you achieve.

Now, let's take a closer look at the creation event once again. Interestingly, the Sovereign Lord could have created everything in one go if He desired to - just a thought and bang, everything would have appeared. Instead, from day one to six, the Creator systematically "made all things" (Colossians 1:16). Have you ever rushed to complete an assignment, a business plan, a project, or anything of value, which at its end failed? If you have, perhaps this was your likely response: 'If only I had spent time… the outcome would have been different.'

Is the Creator teaching humanity a lesson through His systematic structuring of the universe?

Let's look at the sequence of creation to get a better picture. On day one, He called for light and separated it from the darkness. On day two, He separated the oceanic and subterranean waters from the atmospheric waters. On day three, He called dry lands to appear with vegetation, seed-bearing plants, and fruit trees.

On day four, He created the sun, hung it at the centre of the solar system, and then created the moon and stars to orbit it. On day five, he created the creatures of the air and sea. On day six, He created all creatures of the land, small and significant, and lastly, on the same day, he formed man from the dust of the earth. Notice how meticulous and orderly

He was with creation? Nothing was out of place. The Creator's order was order, which He passed unto Adam with the responsibility of maintaining throughout the Earth. Adam was given a specific directive, but he broke the queue, and consequently, chaos entered the world. Since then, disobedient men have continued in disorder. No wonder churches, clergies, homes, schools, industries, governments, families, marriages, and economies are in shambles today. Mankind is out of order!

PERSEVERANCE IS NECESSARY

The best description of perseverance I know is from an old Chinese proverb. It says, "Perseverance is like a battle between a rock and a stream. The stream eventually wins but over time." At the water's surface, the rock appears immovable. However, the water's current over time erodes the rock's foundation. On the surface, it looks like the rock is winning the battle, but it is only a matter of time before it will be able to keep its weight. You must go up against some rocks in life, which, from every indication, seem immovable. However, if you remain persistent, you will become successful over time.

Perseverance is having a never-quit mentality. Though perseverance requires patience, patience is not perseverance.

I describe this as waiting at a terminal while agitated at the long delay.

While patience appreciates the quality of time, perseverance appreciates the worth of time. So don't let the lengthy hold-up discourage you from the journey that awaits. You should strive to persevere because it is worth it - always seeking to be steadfast, immovable, and abounding in the work of the Lord, knowing that your labour in the Lord is not vain - just as a mother in labour feels the discomfort and excruciating pain, yet she still pushes. She knows the pain is worth it. There is gain in your pain. If your perspective is punishment, then all you will feel is pain, but if your perspective is to give birth, then you will endure the pain and be assured of the gain. Isaiah concurs: "For as soon as Zion travailed, she brought forth her children" (Isaiah 66:8). Take careful note that the "brought forth "came from a travailing experience (This is further explained in chapter 12).

If your patience is wearing thin, now is the best time for you to push through.

Like David, who was anointed to become Israel's next king after Saul's rejection, had to labour through thirteen-plus years of trials. David's encounters were preparing him for his ascension.

One important thing that kept David persevering was the worth of God's promise - he knew since God anointed him; it was only a matter of time before He would appoint him.

On this premise, I encourage you to cheer up. Your misfortunes cannot be compared to the glory that you will receive in the end. Your faith is too precious and glorious to be distracted. Continue to press for the prize ahead of time, and at the appointed time, you will be rewarded if you don't faint.

You are not an afterthought. You were in God's plan from day one. Therefore, a delay is not a denial– it is just a matter of the right timing.

Chapter 2
Walking In God's Promises

> He did not waver at the promise of God through unbelief but was strengthened in faith, giving glory to God, 21 and being fully convinced that what He had promised He was also able to perform. Romans 4:20-21

Every Christian must have a total dependency and unwavering confidence in God's word, for He is infallible – whatever He promises, He will fulfil. As you walk with God on the journey of faith, don't lose hope of the promise, but keep striding forward with assurance, being fully persuaded that God has the power to do what he promised.

"For the vision (i.e., the promise), is yet for an appointed time, but at the end, it shall speak and not lie: though it tarry, wait for it, because it will (the guarantee) surely (the assurance) come" (Habakkuk 2:3).

This scripture establishes that God has allocated a set time for the vision to be fulfilled. Many Christians have inconvenienced themselves by allocating their timeline of when they believe the vision must be fulfilled. So, when their desire is not materialized, based on their forecast, they start doubting the One who gave the vision. It will save them a lot of disappointment if they stop trying to give God a helping hand.

Please note that God is not working with man's timing, but man is working with God's timing. Thus, Christians must wait on His timing. And while at it, consider that waiting does not negate the accuracy and surety of the promise. As night follows day, God's pledge is sure. To walk in God's promise requires a few fundamentals:

FAITH ON THE PREMISE OF THE PROMISE

"So then faith cometh by hearing, and hearing by the word of God."

This means that the believer's faith is rooted in the word of God. Since faith and the word of God are intertwined, how can anyone deny the 'isness' of God's promises?

Pastors declare from their pulpits that faith is NOW - substantiating their claim on the first two words in Hebrews

11:1 (Now faith). Such utterance sounds suitable for preaching, but it is not contextual. Firstly, the writer of Hebrews did not state that faith is now. The word 'now' did not correlate with faith in the passage. The word was not used as an adverb but as a conjunction - a transitional word, a bridge that affixes the gap between chapters 10 and 11. Therefore, the premise of what the writer establishes in chapter 10 was concluded in chapter 11. Secondly, if faith is now, that makes yesterday's faith nonexistent and tomorrow's faith obsolete.

Let's resolve what the writer said: "Now faith is..." There you have it! The writer said faith is not now. The word is, as an entity, cannot change, unlike the word now. There are changes in the tenses of is, but its nature remains the same. For example, yesterday it was, today is, and tomorrow is will, but its character remains as is whether it was, is, or will. Hence, you can confidently anchor your faith in God's promise, knowing it is what it is.

According to Paul in Romans 10:17, God's words inspire faith and assure the believers that the Lord is faithful to His words, as He is not slack concerning them. When He says He will bring about His word, He will do it today, yesterday, or tomorrow. So, though your environment may change, God's words remain the same.

Since faith is established on the Lord's "isness", let's wait patiently in expectation of the manifestation of the vision/promise.

GOD'S PROMISES ARE CERTAIN

> "Against all hope, Abraham in hope believed and so became the father of many nations, just as it had been said to him, so shall your offspring be" (Romans 4:18).

Abraham at one point found himself at the intersection of two colliding hopes – a dilemma - one for the promise (word of faith) and the other against the promise (worldly fact). Can you relate to having been in this position, pondering which way to go, contemplating whether to regard the actuality or take a leap of faith? When you come to this crossroads, the promise no longer looks so sure. Coming face to face with unexpected realities makes it challenging to decide which way to go as doubt and confusion set in.

Abraham's faith believed that God would make his name great, but circumstance reminded him that he had no heir. He believed God would make him the father of nations, but biology reminded him that he was an old man. It is a fact that at Abraham's age, he would be unable to get an erection or even maintain one sufficient for intercourse. It was inevitable that Sarah had an ovulation disorder – a blocked fallopian tube rendering her barren. The factor was at her age, fertility would be impossible. From all indications, more incidents were weighted against Abraham and Sarah's faith. The balance was tipped in favour of them giving up, but instead, their faith was lifted. Sometimes, like a balance, the Lord will weigh you down with incidents on one end so He can lift your faith on the other end.

"Therefore, since such a great cloud of witnesses surrounds us, let us lay aside every weight and sin that so easily besets us" (Hebrews 12:1).

Interestingly, the writer urges believers to 'lay aside the weights.' He posits that fleshy weight must be put aside for faith to rise.

God's Promises Are Attainable Goals

The process is generally time-consuming and often requires endurance. Yet, the comforting thing about a process is that it has an end goal. What comes to mind is raw gold put through a fiery procedure that eventually comes out purified. Like gold, believers must be prepared to endure rigorous tasks and tests to attain the goal.

Apostle Paul encouraged the church at Corinth to 'be steadfast, immovable, always abounding in the work of the Lord' (1 Corinthians 15:58). He indicated that eternity with

God should be the believers' ultimate goal. However, this would not be an easy feat; thus, he urged the church to remain focused, knowing that their 'labour is not in vain in the Lord.'

After thirty years of apostolic ministry approaching its end, Paul lived what he preached and was eventually rewarded for his labour. He affirmed his resilience by declaring, "I have fought a good fight, I have finished the course, and I have kept the faith" (2 Timothy 4:7). He identifies faith as a belief, a journey, and a daily fight. The Greek word for fight speaks of a contest for victory or mastery. It describes the evangelical contest against the enemies of man's salvation. The word illustrates the straining of one's nerves to achieve the goal.

Paul was determined to be heaven-bound he declares;

> "I want to know Christ and the power of His resurrection and the fellowship of sharing in His suffering, becoming like Him in His death, and so, somehow to attain the resurrection from the dead" (Philippians 3:10).

A commentary puts it like this, "Paul already knew Christ as his Savior, but he wanted to know Him more intimately as his Lord." To 'know' denotes knowledge gleaned through intimate experience with God - not the kind handed down by oral tradition. To honestly know God requires true intimacy with Him. However, as stated previously, this kind comes with much suffering. Thus, the believers, through suffering for Christ's sake, will experience the power of His resurrection.

Paul also asserts, "Not that I have already obtained all this, or have already been made perfect, but I press on to take hold of that for which Christ Jesus took hold of me. Brothers, I do not consider myself yet to have taken hold of it. But one thing I do: forgetting what is behind and straining toward what is ahead." Paul, with all his accolades and spiritual accomplishments, could have boasted about his achievements, but instead, he saw them as meaningless without Christ. Spiritual accomplishment without commitment and a faithful relationship with the Lord does not guarantee a place in the afterlife. Personal accomplishment is good, but without a spiritual walk, it is nothing. Paul told the believers that he had not yet attained the main prize but was still actively pressing toward it. Sadly, many have taken their eyes off the prize the moment they achieve their personal goals. The Apostle's testimony should remind us that earthly achievements, while exemplary, are not the final stage - spiritual growth is better. With all of God's promises, do not forget He also promises eternal life. Heaven must be your ultimate goal; it is worth more than personal success. While attaining what you can on Earth is wise, it must not come at the expense of losing out on heaven.

THE PAST
(FORGET THE THINGS THAT ARE BEHIND)

People often chastise themselves for things they did before they were saved, but it doesn't have to be that way. After all, the people who did those awful things no longer exist.

The scripture states, 'forget the things that are behind.' In other words, do not allow your past to affect you now. While you cannot change your past, you can change how you respond to the past. It is wise not to let past failures stop you from going forward. To have a terrible past is wrong, but it is worse not to have learned anything from it.

There is danger in looking back, for it halts progress. Those affected by it create monuments rather than making movements - always remembering but never learning.

You perhaps have met these kinds of people – the ones who are constantly reminding you of what things used to be.

The late Baptist preacher, John Claypool, once told a story of two Buddhist monks walking in a thunderstorm. They came to a swollen stream. A beautiful young Japanese woman in a kimono stood there, wanting to cross to the other side but afraid of the currents. One of the monks said,

"Can I help you?" "I need to cross this stream," replied the woman. The monk picked her up, put her on his shoulder, carried her through the swirling waters, and put her down on the other side. He and his companion then went on to the monastery. That night, his companion said to him, "I have a bone to pick with you. As Buddhist monks, we have taken vows not to look at a woman, much less touch her body. Back there by the river, you did both." "My brother," answered the other monk, "I put that woman down on the other side of the river. You're still carrying her in your mind." See how easy it is to be obsessed with the past at the expense of the future? Dwelling on the past will not get you anywhere. Accept it; you cannot change what has already been done (unless you can time travel). However, with your walk with God, you can make adjustments as He orders your steps in the now and heal you from your past pain.

THE PRESENT
(UTMOST STRAIN TOWARDS THE GOAL)

An athlete in a race has one objective: to competitively make it across the finish line. The walk of faith can be described as an intense training routine for a main event.

The preparations are demanding, but an athlete who desires the prize will strain every nerve to do what is required.

Can you honestly say you are 'straining' to reach the goal? For many people, the journey of faith is a hit-or-miss proposition. When they succeed, they praise the Lord. But when they fail, they complain to the Lord. Such an attitude will get them nowhere. Being content with sitting around and waiting for life to hand you the prize will be a cold day in hell. So quit sitting around and start pressing toward the mark. 'Mark' refers to the 'goal one has in view.' Oblivious to its surroundings but focusing on the prize. Many have gone to the blocks primed and excited to go but, after a few missteps, have fallen out of the race. On the track of life, always seek to endure to the end regardless of the blunders.

God is pleased by a race well run and a life well lived. You can look back like a triumphant athlete and say, "I did well!" While bearing in mind how well you ran and finished with the aid of the Holy Spirit as your instructor. Therefore, never cease to make Him the priority in your run of faith.

THE FUTURE (LOOKING FORWARD TO THE PRIZE)

There is an overwhelming feeling when one sees all their hard work and effort have paid off. The moment encourages reflection on the obstacles conquered, and with a jubilant smile, one declares, "I have made it!" Likewise, amid torrid encounters, always strive to make heaven your final destination.

Your labour and self-sacrifice are for the future life with your Lord that awaits you. Let's recount the words of Paul: "I have fought the good fight, I have finished the race, I have kept the faith." In case you haven't noticed, Paul's reflection was in the past tense – experiences he encountered – circumstances he had been through. May his testimony serve to remind you that faith's journey comes with challenges, but it will be a good fight. How do you know the fight is good? You know when all the challenges are over, and you are still standing. The antagonist of the saints is a vile adversary, so to come out standing is a fight well fought. Thus, you can reflect, as Paul did, and testify, 'I have fought a good fight.'

God cannot lie. Therefore, whatever He promises over your life, He will perform it. Let not your trust in His word waver but build it on the premise of His promise.

Chapter 3
It Will Be OK

For I reckon that the sufferings of this present time are not worthy to be compared with the glory which shall be revealed in us. Romans 18:8

The church is called into a relationship with the Lord. Like all relationships, a key component needed is trust. When trust is not an integral part of a relationship, it leads to adverse effects such as lack of communication. The believers' trust in the Lord is not gauged by trials but by His words. The faithful saint will not refrain from communicating with the Lord, even when faced with trials. When the Lord says He will do something, be assured it will be done, for He honours His word above His name. With this in mind, the believers can be comforted knowing that it (whatever it is) will be ok! This is a declaration of faith, not a mere statement.

THE BIBLICAL DIMENSIONS OF FAITH:

1. **Faith is a walk** – by it, the believers walk (not by sight). 2. **Faith is a talk** – by it, the believers make their request known. 3. Faith comes by hearing – the believers hear and believe the Word of God. 4. Faith is a lifestyle – by it, the just shall live. In a nutshell, the Word of God encourages believers to walk by faith, talk by faith, hear by faith, and live by faith. Essentially, the believers are to walk, talk, hear, and live by faith because it is interwoven with the promises of God. Therefore, do not forget the promises of God, though you may be bombarded with problems. Take heed to this wise saying, praise always takes precedence over problems because praise declares God's sovereignty, and therefore, no problem is more significant than Him. In the book of Isaiah (54:1), Israel was instructed to 'sing' in her 'barren' state. Her breakthrough from the predicament was hinged on praise. Additionally, praise sets the tone for what is to come. It is pretty simple: failure to trust God does not make Him any less of who He is, but he who fails to trust the Lord is made less. So, stop whining and be faithful to the end.

Abraham, the father of faith, had many personal challenges, yet he exuded absolute confidence in the Lord that He could do that which was humanly impossible. The Lord promised

Abraham he would give him and Sarah a child and innumerable posterity. However, they were both advanced in age when he received this promise. Yet, Abraham and Sarah had absolute confidence that the Lord could do it. From mankind's perspective, it is impossible, but from the Divine position, nothing is impossible. The faith of Abraham and Sarah demonstrates to the believers that when they place complete trust in the Lord, they will be rewarded, as the 'Lord can do exceedingly abundantly above all that they ask or think, according to the power that works in them' (Ephesians 3:20).

In context, Abraham made the non-meritorious decision to walk by faith, talk by faith, hear by faith, and live by faith in trusting the Lord to deliver on His promise to give him not only an heir from his own body but also innumerable descendants, even while he was yet childless.

Like Abraham, be encouraged; though your environment and experiences are visibly contrary to the promise given by the Lord, He is not slack concerning His covenant – it is yea and amen.

OATH OF GOD

When the Lord gave His promise to Abraham since there was no one greater for Him to swear by, He swore by

Himself and confirmed it with an oath (Read Hebrews 6). An oath was a legal verbal contract that bound the swearer to his/her pledge by swearing to something or someone greater than him/herself. Since God is infallible, there was nothing or no one He could swear by but Himself, thus cementing the unshakable premise that His promises are ultimately trustworthy.

Therefore, believers can trust the promises because the Promiser is not slack concerning them. There may be extended delays, but this does not indicate that He will fall short of his vow. It is a natural reaction to surmise that someone who has pledged has forgotten or cannot fulfil their obligation after waiting a long time. However, no such inference can be drawn with God, as time is not a factor to Him. Therefore, He never forgets – He doesn't suffer from Alzheimer's, nor will He fail to fulfil His obligations.

APPRECIATE DELAYS

God is not a man but a Supreme Being who cannot lie. With this truth, the believers should be encouraged to stay the course and not be disheartened and impatient, regardless of the intervals. Believers must learn to appreciate them as intermissions for reflection, introspection and drawing closer to the Lord.

I am convinced that God allows delays for His children to draw closer to Him. The longer gold is spent in the fire, the better it becomes. So, appreciate the Lord's delays by seeing them as breakthroughs instead of breakdowns. With such confidence, the believers should be able to say, as James did, "I count it all joy when I fall into diverse temptation" (James 1:2) because the trying of the believers' faith produces perseverance. Do not become a spoiled child who rants at God when He delays the blessings but gives Him no praise when He relays them.

When a promise is given, it incites expectation on the part of the receiver. This assurance anchor is why many are still holding onto their firm belief. Promise inspires conviction, and conviction ignites hope. Hope is like a door that hinges on the doorpost of promise. If the door is moved, you still have a doorpost standing. However, if the doorpost is moved, there is no structure to hold up the door. Thus, the Believer's hope is useless if it has no structural post to hold it up. Their expectation is driven and held together by the promise of God. Their desires must hinge on the doorpost of His promise. With this assurance, the believers can remain calm amid the chaos around them.

VALUE IN DISAPPOINTMENTS

Norman Vincent Peale once said, *"The believers must turn their disappointment to God-appointment, as sometimes life's disappointments are positive developments of God's plan."*

Disappointment is a vicious and debilitating enemy. It can cause emotional disturbances that lead to a loss of trust, which causes people to shun those who genuinely want to help. Because disappointment can strike at almost any time, believers need to learn to deal with it.

Life has its fair share of rough and tough times, but the faithful, in the end, will overcome them. Therefore, do not allow disappointments and struggles to shake your belief in the goodness and promises of God. "Do not throw away your confidence, which has a great reward" (Hebrews 10:35).

IT WILL BE OKAY

Paul had a struggle in his flesh that he described as a 'thorn' (Read Romans 12:7-10). Three times, he asked the Lord to move it. On his third attempt, the Lord answered and told him no! Instead, the Lord offered Paul His grace to sustain him. An unlikely response for one who is requesting deliverance, isn't it? But Paul's reaction is worthy of commendation - it was a testament to his faithfulness. He recognized that the Lord's strength would be made perfect in his weakness and so declared,

> "Most gladly, therefore, will I rather glory in my infirmities, that the power of Christ may rest upon me. Therefore, I take pleasure in infirmities, reproaches, necessities, persecutions, distresses for Christ's sake: for when I am weak, then am I strong" (2 Corinthians 12:8-10).

Like Paul, when the believers start acknowledging the Lord's grace as strength to be made perfect in them, they will stop complaining about their thorns. Seize the moments to worship, knowing your trial is a testament to where you are going. In the words of Paul,

> "For I reckon, the suffering of this present time is not worthy to be compared with the glory that shall be revealed in us" (Romans 8:18).

You don't have to see where you are going as long as He who has given the promise is exceedingly, abundantly, above, and more than able to see it through. Thank the Lord for all He has done and given you instead of whining about what He has not done. Always be thankful to God, knowing He will grant your desires - it will be okay.

Failure to trust God does not make Him less of who He is. But your failure to trust Him will make you less in Him. So, stop whining and be faithful to the end. In the end, it will be okay.

Chapter 4
I Am Purposed

"Now Israel loved Joseph more than all his children because he was the son of his old age: and he made him a coat of many colors." Genesis 37:3

Have you ever considered your life meaningless and pondered 'Who am I' rather than affirming 'Who am I?' Do you believe achievement is heavily based on experience and that social background determines status? Some people conclude that their lives are meaningless due to their backgrounds. However, being alive is a testament that one's life is valuable and serves a purpose.

One character who overcame his toxic environs to elevate to the top of the game was Joseph. He flourished in whatever conditions he found himself in - the pit, Potiphar's house and prison. People of purpose will survive in any hostile environment and make it their own. In other words, their environment doesn't affect them, but they leave a lasting effect there. The sooner you identify your purpose, the sooner you see that your life is meaningful.

WHAT IS PURPOSE?

The purpose is to know exactly where to go and how to get there. It is pretty simple – you can't honestly see your purpose until you know where you are going and how to get there. Purpose is like your identity; if you don't know it, you won't know what you are. You become lost in who you are, where you are going, and why you are here. Purpose is often used interchangeably with destiny. Even though there are similarities, the two are distinctive. If you picture life as a journey, then destiny is the terminus, and purpose is the route (with its occasional 'pit stops') that gets you there. In other words, destiny is where you are going, and purpose is knowing how you get there. Until you truly know who you are, you won't truly know where you are going. The most significant opposition to purpose is fear. You cannot know what you are gifted at if you fear trying anything.

ILLUSTRATIONS OF PURPOSE

The story of Joseph is the best to illustrate the dynamics of purpose. As we look into the life of Joseph, we can see ourselves through his life – his affliction, hatred, betrayal, incarceration, regret, bitterness, deliverance, and prominence. Let's look at several illustrations of purpose from one of our favourite Bible characters:

PURPOSE IS NOT INFLUENCED BY POSITION (GENESIS 37:3)

Straightaway, we see why Jacob loved Joseph more than his brethren – Jacob had him when he was aged. Joseph was the son of Rachel (Jacob's favourite wife), who was barren. Perhaps Jacob had given up hope that Rachel would give him any children, especially in his old age, until a miracle, Joseph, was conceived. Imagine the joy Jacob felt having a son in his old age and from the wife he truly loved and desired. So, Jacob showed more love for Joseph than his other sons. The reason was apparent, even if the readers disagreed with Jacob's blatant favouritism. What is especially interesting about this story is that Rachel eventually had another son named Benjamin. Therefore, this meant that Jacob had Benjamin at an older age than when he had Joseph. Thus, Benjamin (since he was the last born), not Joseph, should have been given the coat. Joseph was not the youngest (according to his birth position), yet he was the most loved. Jacob's affection for Joseph testifies that purpose is not influenced by position.

In today's social structure, a promotion is evident by moving up in position. But God does not have to move you out of position to promote you. He will favour you right where you are, as the only position God is interested in is the heart. Therefore, remain faithful - your Father will elevate you right where you are.

PURPOSE CANNOT BE HIDDEN
(GENESIS 37:3,18)

People of purpose always stand out, regardless of their position, place or predicament. After being sold into Egypt, Joseph stood out in Potiphar's house, in prison and before Pharaoh.

Jacob had made a coat of many colours for Joseph. Please note the coat was not made of one material printed in many colours but one made of twelve materials of different colours. This showed Jacob's time and patience in weaving the coat and giving it to Joseph was particular. Joseph's brothers knew of the coat's significance, which was one reason they despised him. Perhaps his brothers would not have had an issue with the coat if it were plain. The brothers despised him because he was colourful, making him stand out.

When his brothers were around, they looked ordinary in their plain coats. Joseph, in his unique coat, was visible even from afar (Genesis 37:18). His brothers saw him from a distance and knew for sure it was him because of the apparent coat he had on. Have you ever wondered why you are constantly being called upon? It could be that you are graced with favour and stand out.

PURPOSE INCITES THE HATERS (FEAR FEARS FAVOR) (GENESIS 37:4-8, 18-20)

Joseph's coat symbolises favour, yet it inflamed envy from his brothers. In addition to the coat, his brothers hated him, for he was a dreamer and was loved the most by their father. Though he was their brother, he was treated like an outcast, and they conspired to kill him. Remember these sound words - not everyone is/will be enthused about your mantle and vision. some will conspire to rip the mantle off you and stop the vision. That is precisely what Joseph's brothers did to him – stripped him of his coat, tore it into pieces, and then cast him into a pit to die.

Their initial words were, "Let us kill him and see what becomes of his dream." The brothers' actions revealed the magnitude of which they feared the favour of Joseph's life.

Their main fear was Joseph's dream. They aimed to deny the dream – the only way it could be done was to kill the dreamer. You know you are envied when others seek to eliminate you without reason.

After which, they put Joseph in a pit and had a feast. Sadly, this is a reflection of what takes place in Christendom today. Some people only celebrate (feast) when those they despise are absent. They see the gifted as a threat and fear the favour upon their life because the mantle makes them stand out.

Such envy has driven many humble saints to refrain from wearing the Father's mantle to avoid becoming targets. But why should anyone stop wearing the mantle because others don't like how it looks on them?

THOUGH YOU CARRY IT, DON'T BREAK PROTOCOL (GENESIS 37:10-11)

I have seen many people need clarification on their gifts with being designated in ministry. Being gifted does not readily mean you are called to pastor a church or lead a movement. One factor affecting the body of Christ is that too many self-proclaimed gifted individuals are elevating themselves in positions not designated for them. They have allowed their giftedness to go straight to their heads.

Joseph was gifted in interpreting dreams and would eventually be Pharaoh's right-hand man to preserve his brethren (Israel) from an impending famine. However, note God Himself orchestrated Joseph's installation. Those who faithfully wait on God Almighty will be elevated, even amid adversity.

Joseph told his brothers of his dreams, angered them because they understood their meanings. One day, his father was among his brothers when he reported one of the dreams. His father rebuked him when he was finished but observed the dream. Since Jacob observed the dream, why did he rebuke Joseph? I have heard the speculation that Jacob was jealous of his son's dream. I, on the other hand, believe Jacob's rebuke was not one of ill intent. The fact that he observed the dream indicates he had no problem with the dream. However, he had a problem with how Joseph presented the dream. Joseph announced, amid his brothers, that Jacobi would bow before him. The manner was not honourable and deserving of the rebuke. Joseph should have shown his father respect by proclaiming the dream privately to him. Despite Joseph's purpose, being gifted is no excuse to break protocol. Until you have been designated, wait!

PURPOSE IN THE PIT (GENESIS 37:18-28)

Purpose only dies when the holder refuses it. His brothers cast him into the pit to decide what to do with him. It is noticeable that Joseph was cast into an empty pit. Thus, when they cast him in, he became its occupant. I believe God will sometimes allow you to be cast into an empty situation for you to fill it. So, instead of complaining about the emptiness, ask yourself, 'What is my assignment?' I have concluded that people of purpose are born to fill voids; the onus is theirs to find what they are.

After contemplating what to do with Joseph, his brothers decided to sell him to Egypt. So, they lifted him 'up' and 'out' of the pit. Conversely, the same hands that tried to bury him became the hands that lifted him up and out. Some people who tried to bury you will eventually know your price (Joseph's was 20 pieces of silver). Joseph could not have been lifted 'up' and 'out' if he had not been put down and in. So many people desire the 'up' and 'out' experience but complain about the down and the ordeal. The only way to come up and out is if one goes down and in. Except if a grain of wheat is buried, it cannot spring forth. Joseph's brothers had no clue that their ill will towards him, putting him down in a hole had a prophetic implication. By burying Joseph in the pit, they planted a seed to deliver them from an impending dreadful famine.

PURPOSE PROVIDES PROVISION
(GENESIS 37:12-17)

God sees mankind's evil intentions toward His children and will always provide a way out for them. "No weapon formed against thee shall prosper, and every tongue rises against thee shall be condemned" (Isaiah 54:17). "Surely He shall deliver you from the snare of the fowler and the noisome pestilence" (Psalm 91:3). God ultimately has His children's back.

God provided ways of escape for Joseph. It was not coincidental that his brothers left Shechem and went to Dothan. If they had stayed in Shechem, Joseph would probably have drowned, as the wells in Shechem were likely full of water. Thus, God provided an empty pit in Dothan.

It was not coincidental that the merchants passed through Dothan on their way to Egypt. Joseph would not have been sold to the merchants if the brothers had stayed in Shechem. As a child of God, you don't always understand the strange things happening to you, but in the grand finale, you will see how things are adding up for your good. So, despite all the turmoil you are experiencing, remain faithful. In the end, you will see its purpose.

FROM PURPOSE TO PURPOSE

From a multi-coloured coat to a royal robe. Joseph's coat symbolized God's grace upon his life. His jealous brothers tore the coat his father gave him to pieces. Sadly, not everyone likes the grace that is on you - they are fuming with envy and wish to strip you of the mantle.

While Joseph's brothers uncovered his coat, given by his father, it was strangers (Potiphar and Pharaoh) who covered him with another. Strangers may know your value more than your own. Some of your kind will seek ways to break you down. Thank God for those He assigned in your life to build you up.

Joseph was covered three times: by his father (Israel), his master (Potiphar), and his king (Pharaoh).

The three coats symbolize three stages of Joseph's life – the promise, the process, and the purpose. When our Father gives His promise, we can be confident that he will bring it to purpose. However, we know this cannot happen without process. Joseph, the promised son, had to be a servant to

Potiphar and a slave in prison before he could get to his purpose in the palace.

Be encouraged, and don't allow misfortune and rejection to make you think your life is insignificant. Stop equating your challenges to having little or no significance. Even in the pit (obscurity, darkness, loneliness), you are still a son or daughter of purpose.

The Apostle Paul once said, "The sufferings of this present time are not worthy to be compared with the glory that shall be revealed unto you" (Romans 8:18). Paul encourages faithful believers to recognize that current mishaps or misfortunes are nothing compared to what awaits the faithful. Therefore, encountering misfortunes or mishaps is not the problem – it lies within the response. You can either let the mischances build or break you. Pause for a while and consider your response – break or make? The positive outcome depends on your faithfulness and commitment during the test. Quit asking, who am I? And start declaring, I am!

REQUIREMENTS/NECESSITIES OF PURPOSE

FAITH: Growing up in church, I was taught that fear is a spirit. I substantiated this with scriptures but also found out that this spirit is the absence of faith. Therefore, it will be impossible to please God without faith. Fear has crippled many people from stepping into their purpose. The fear of failing and not being good enough will make an individual miss a prospective opportunity to fulfil their purpose. One will never know his purpose until he decides to step out by faith - like a trapezist must trust his partner before taking that leap of faith in mid-air to catch him. Likewise, we trust God to make our leap of faith. Trust in God is very important in getting you to your destination. It is like the sheep that must trust the shepherd to take it to its destination safely. We don't always know or see where we are going, but we trust our Lord to take us there. This is called faith.

IDENTITY: A man without a sense of purpose is a man without an identity. It does not matter how often others validate and affirm his greatness; he will not know and only sees himself as a failure and alone. A quote I picked states, "Loneliness is not the absence of people; it is the absence of purpose." If you do not know the answer to who you are, you will not know what you are capable of.

TIMING: The Bible says that there will be seedtime and harvest as long as the earth remains. (Genesis 8:22). Note they do not come simultaneously. Seedtime, then harvest and harvest, then seedtime - a recurring cycle. So, there may be a good reason you have yet to see a harvest - it is yet to be time. So quit complaining and keep sowing. Galatians 6:9 tells us to 'be not weary in doing well for we shall reap in due season if we faint not.' The Apostle Paul uses the agricultural analogy to express the importance of timing. A farmer does not sow a seed today and expects to reap immediately tomorrow. The farmer knows there is a process between sowing and reaping called toiling. Toiling is not an easy process, yet the farmer is unwilling to be weary of the process, as his ultimate goal is to reap from the harvest.

It is interesting to note the term 'in due season' means a specific time. Not all crops carry the same season; some are common while others are uncommon - their seasons vary. If you are asking God, why is my time taking so long? Now you know it could be that what has been planted for you is uncommon and requires a specific time.

DECLARATION: You will only step into your purpose once you start declaring what the Word says you are. "Be not conform to this world but be transformed by the renewing of your mind" (Romans 12:1). a defeated mindset is already a defeated outcome. Start declaring and affirming over your life what the word of God says you are. Quit labelling yourself as insignificant, inferior, unintelligent, substandard, unattractive, and unsuccessful. Say it aloud:

"I am not a failure! I had to win a race just to be born. I am here because I was the first to reach my mother's egg. Since I won that race to be here, I refuse to quit now that I am here. A winning nature is in me!"

"I am Blessed!"

"I am More Than a Conqueror!" "I am Royalty!"

"I am Special!" "I am Peculiar!"

"I am a Child of a King!" "I am the Head!"

"I am Prosperous!" "I am Beautiful!" "I am Successful!" "I am Victorious!" "I am Gifted!"

God says, "I know the plans I have for you, plans for welfare and not for evil, to give you a future hope." Amen.

SEED: A seed can be money as well as stewardship. As you give faithfully and know you are sowing into your destiny, you wait patiently for maturity to see the fruit of your labour. Remember, no one goes to the bank to withdraw without having made any deposit. Paul told Timothy, a gifted young man, to stir what was in him. The most significant seed you can sow in yourself is the one that stirs your gift. Being dormant and not making any deposit in the area of your strengths, desires, and gifts will only leave you an empty shell of your true potential. Don't be naïve. While sowing in other people, things, and areas, don't forget to sow in your dreams, gifts, and aspirations.

PROCESS: When the goldsmith puts the raw material through the furnace, his purpose is to purify the material. The way to bring it to that purpose is through fire. A person of purpose will go through a process. Do not run from it; just embrace it. Running from the process is blatantly running from purpose. Embrace and acknowledge it. It is designed to make you stronger and more efficient for the task ahead.

MANIFESTATIONS: Purpose must be seen; it must be visible. You have yet to attain your purpose if no one can see it. Purpose cannot be hidden – if you are the only one seeing it, it's just a desire. The purpose of Elijah's servant, Elisha, was seen – he did twice the number of miracles as his predecessor.

SERVITUDE: (Water for Oil) When Elijah first met Elisha in the field, he threw his mantle over him and walked away. As we know, this was symbolic of the transference of the prophetic office on Elisha.

Knowing what the gesture meant, Elisha could have continued with business as usual, but instead, he left the field and became Elijah's close attendant. For several years,

Elisha poured water into Elijah's hands, and in return, Elijah poured oil on his head. Many Christians today want oil pouring on them but are unwilling to be water pourers. The oil is costly; are you willing to work/serve for it?

Purpose is your identity. Without it, you will not know who you are and where you are going. Your fear of finding it will therefore be your detriment.

Chapter 5
Help

"The impotent man answered Him, Sir, I have no man, when the water is troubled, to put me into the pool."
John 5:7

Everyone needs help at some point in their lives. The problem, however, is that help, especially a good one, is hard to find. How discouraging it is to desire help, but only some are willing to offer it? Especially considering how quick you are to aid others. In such a position, it is easy to focus on who is not helping rather than appreciating the helpers. In this story, we learn of a crippled man who almost missed help (from Jesus) because he was so preoccupied with not having any help.

The Jews believed that at a particular time of the year, an angel would come down at the pool of Bethesda to trouble the water, giving it curative powers, and whoever got into the water first would be cleansed from their condition. As a result, many sick people of various conditions would gather at the pool for the 'troubling of the water.' The people were from all walks of life - a testament that no one is immune to misfortunes. So please delete the absurd thinking that you are the only person encountering one.

The crowd that gathered at the pool consisted of people from diverse backgrounds, yet had three things in common that every man can relate to:

CONDITION

They all had a condition – they were blind, deaf, and paralyzed and gathered under the colonnades, waiting for the water to be troubled. The truth is everyone has conditions. The difference is that we don't always share the same kind. Identifying and labelling other people's conditions when you have a kind of your own is wrong. The problem is not that the condition exists; it is denying that you have one. There is a word for this – hypocrisy. The Greek hypokrites is a stage performer who plays a character on stage. His true identity is hidden behind the mask. Jesus sarcastically puts it like this, 'remove the beam out of your eye so that you can see the speck in your brother's eye.' A beam was used as a post to hold up a structure, e.g., in a house or roof. This is what Jesus illustrates to be in the eye of a hypocrite. The speck is a tiny splinter from the beam.

Yet, only a hypocrite (according to Jesus) has the powerful eyesight to see it in another person's eye - the kind of people who like to call out other people's conditions while theirs is a mess.

The first step in being delivered from a condition is admitting that you have one. "Confess your sins, and He will be faithful and just to forgive you and cleanse you from all unrighteousness" (1 John 1:9).

Also, it is worth mentioning that the people who gathered that day were all together, and none esteemed himself/herself above the other - they all had a common denominator, a condition.

They all waited — they sat, lay under the colonnades, and waited for the water to be troubled. We all can attest to waiting for a word, a breakthrough, a miracle, a deliverance, etc. This can be frustrating, especially when it's been a long time. Isaiah writes, "They that wait upon the Lord shall renew their strength" (Isaiah 40:31). Waiting is processing, and therefore, anything that is unprocessed will not meet the standard. A mother has to wait for the due process to give birth; anything before that time is considered premature. Do not interrupt the process because you cannot wait for the due process.

You will never find a mother in the maternity ward with her legs in the stirrup smiling while in labour. You will never find her looking down there, making baby faces to the child she is bringing forth. Instead, whilst still in pain, she is concerned about her child - playful moments can come after. Paul, to the Corinthians, writes,

> "Be ye steadfast, immovable, always abounding in the work of the Lord knowing this, that your labour is not in vain"
> (1 Corinthians 15:58).

A mother pushes, even though she is in agony because she knows her labour is not in vain. After delivery, she forgets about the ordeal.

Many people do not like waiting and want God to expedite the process. But believers must learn to be patient and understand that their waiting is part of the process. The people at the colonnades all knew that they had to wait. They knew the season of the angel's troubling of the water, but none knew the exact time it would happen. Therefore, they waited.

They all needed help – John was specific in describing the people; they were blind, lame, and paralyzed. They would need an aide to guide them to the pool based on their conditions.

A man with a condition for thirty-eight years was waiting at the pool. When Jesus saw him there, He asked the man if he needed to be whole. At first glance, it appears Jesus' question was ridiculous, as the only reason the man was out was so he could be healed of his condition. Since the man's condition was apparent, why did Jesus ask the question? I submit to you that there is more to the question. Let's look at the passage in context.

Firstly, Jesus singled out the man, why? According to John's account, the crowd was innumerable (multitude), so why, of all the people there, did Jesus select him? What was unique about him? Jesus visibly saw that he had no aide. The man said, "I have no one to help me when the water is troubled."

DROPPED

I find it perplexing that this man had no one to help him into the pool as he had to get initial help to be at the location, considering that he was paralyzed. His helpers only dropped him off and left. Have you ever been in that position where others offered to help you all the way but only left you part of the way? The paralyzed man was frustrated at not having any help, thus his angry response to Jesus.

Another character that relates to being dropped is Mephibosheth. At a tender age, his nurse tumbled and subsequently broke both his legs. How ironic is that? The person in charge of his care was responsible for 'breaking' him.

What do the man at the pool and Mephibosheth have in common apart from being dropped? Both their minds were still intact. If you lose anything, don't lose your mind because you will need it for the opportune time. For the man at the pool, it was Jesus' word: 'Rise, take up your bed, and walk.' It required his presence of mind to do as Jesus instructed him. For Mephibosheth, it was his presence of mind to respond to David's call.

EMPOWERED TO DO IT YOURSELF

Jesus asked the man, "Do you want to be made whole?" He replied, "I have no one to help me." Instead of answering the question, the man complained about his predicament and subsequently misunderstood Jesus' true intent for asking the question – which was to help him. Individuals preoccupied with their conditions are usually blind to recognizing help when it arrives.

Jesus told him to rise, take up his bed, and walk. In other words, Jesus helped him by empowering him to help himself. He had been looking for help from others when all he needed was to help himself.

Have you ever considered that in some instances, God did NOT allow others to help you because they would have taken the glory for themselves, attributing your success to their involvement? While I believe that the Lord will assign people to other people's lives, I also believe He will empower people to help themselves. That way, no one can claim His glory.

The lame man was told to 'rise,' which was previously impossible. Likewise, may the Lord empower you to rise from your conditions.

'Take up your bed' – the thing he was confined to is now in his control. Likewise, may you have power over the things you were once confined to. The lame man was brought on a bed, but he left carrying his bed - symbolizing total control of things he was once bound to. He was also instructed to 'walk' so that everyone who witnessed his breakthrough would know it was not a lucky break. Likewise, the naysayers will witness the hand of the Lord upon your life.

Reflection

Nothing is wrong with desiring help from others. But there will come occasions when the Lord equips you to help yourself. Don't miss those opportunities by still procrastinating.

Chapter 6
Possessing A Winning Mindset

"I press toward the mark for the prize of the high calling of God in Christ Jesus."
Philippians 3:14

It is said a winner never quits, and a quitter never wins. The expression is a testament to the fact that hard work and determination are vital in acquiring and maintaining success. I agree! A Jamaican proverb that corroborates says, "If yuh waan good, yuh nose haffi run." This contradicts the misguided belief that successful people are only those who have attended top-league learning institutions, and success is only bestowed to those born in luxury or, as the saying goes, 'with a gold spoon in their mouths.'

The common denominator contributing to failure is passivity. Everyone has goals they would like to accomplish. However, making them a reality is more than wishful thinking. It requires discipline, commitment, and obedience. Failure to make any attempt at success is already a failure of mindset. Shakespeare once said, "Some people are born great, some achieve greatness, and others have greatness thrust upon them." However, regardless of what manner greatness comes, maintaining it will require intent action. Therefore, the benchmark of success is work, work, work, and more work.

Hard work eventually pays off, as opposed to doing nothing at all. Anyone with lackadaisical thinking will never be successful - even if they attain some substance, it will be short-lived.

On that note, there are two types of thinkers in the world:

THE POSITIVE THINKER

-One who is fearless in taking on challenges, even if he fails in his attempt. His indomitable spirit will not allow him to quit.

THE NEGATIVE THINKER

– this is the naysayer – the one whose view of the task is insurmountable and, therefore, quits without an attempt at trying.

Have you considered which of the two you are? Do you see the destination halfway ahead or halfway behind?

If you constantly see yourself as one step behind instead of a step ahead, you will never attempt to do what needs to be done to improve your life. Seeking success without any will to work is like a working vehicle always parked in the driveway – it will not move by itself. Take a risk; jump in and drive! You just might travel somewhere you always wanted to go. Trying something new or a different approach is not bad, and even if you fail at the onset, don't be discouraged; see it as a lesson learned to do better next time.

SUCCESS

Success is not just a motion; it is also a mentality. Mental fortitude is as vital as motion in climbing the uphill ladder of achievement. A weak mindset will crumble under failure, but a fortified mind, even with failed attempts, learns from every experience. Don't ever see failures as final – see them as steps bringing you closer to your destination.

Experience teaches that only crazy-minded people repeat the same things and expect to get different results. It is as if they are either bonkers or afraid to make changes.

Only some changes are reasonable. One morning, Jesus told His disciples to return to sea after they had been toiling all night and caught nothing. Considering their fishing experience, perhaps they felt Jesus' request insulted their expertise. However, against all they knew, the disciples, notably Simon, were willing to do something different. His words were, "Nevertheless, at your word, Lord." Simon might have been uncertain that Jesus' instruction would work and may have thought to himself it could not get any worse than the event earlier. Frankly speaking, Simon and the others had nothing to lose. If, after several attempts at the same thing without any result, what would it cost to do something different? Absolutely nothing! The disciples decided to do something different, and their result was different – they caught so many fish that the net was broken. See, sitting around waiting for something to happen will not make it happen - It is better to do something than to do nothing if you desire tangible results.

A Bible story I find befitting about taking action where necessary tells the tale of four lepers who sat outside Israel's gate during a great famine. One said to the others, "If we sit here, we will all die, but if we march in the direction of our enemies, they may spare our lives." The rationale behind the thought is that if the enemy spared their lives, the worst that could happen is that they would be enslaved. As slaves, they would be given scrappy food to eat, but it beats dying from starvation sitting outside their city's gate.

In their minds, it was better to launch out on a 'half-full' possibility than to sit around on a 'half-empty' impossibility. Which half are you holding unto? In your decision lies the difference between you winning or losing.

"Unsuccessful people focus their thinking on survival, ordinary people focus their thinking on maintenance, and successful people focus their thinking on progress," says John C. Maxwell. You must understand that success comes to those who habitually do things that unsuccessful people don't do. The more purposeful you see yourself, the more possibilities you can achieve. As Victor Hugo and René Descartes asserted, "An invasion of armies can be resisted, but not an invasion of ideas." "The mind, while it may live in the brain, is a mere non-material thing, separate from the grey mass of tissue that surrounds it. I think, therefore, I am."

A significant percentage of achieving your goal is knowing what you want and pressing towards it. I find the life of the late singer/musician Ray Charles Robinson exceptionally motivating and inspiring for those who think reaching their goal is unattainable. Charles, at the age of five, witnessed his brother's death – he had fallen into a washtub and drowned. Two years later, he lost his sight and, shortly after that, experienced the tragic loss of his mother. Before Charles' mother passed away, she encouraged her blind son not to give up on fulfilling his dream to become a musician.

Driven by his mother's words, Charles could take the losses of his brother, sight and mother and use them as extraordinary positives in pursuing his passion of becoming a musician. Today, Ray Charles is renowned and considered one of the musical greats of all time.

I use the words of Voltaire, to sum up best Charles's great legacy: "Great men are those who excel at creating pure and lasting pleasure for something yet to be born. The plunderers of the provinces are merely heroes. With me, great comes first and heroes last."

GREAT DIFFERENCE

The critical difference between possessing a winner mindset and a quitter mindset is that the former sees themselves at the edge of a breakthrough. In contrast, the latter see themselves at the edge of despair. A great thinker is more focused on completing and accessing the prize at the end of the task rather than focusing on the ills and turmoil. However, with that said, God Himself is the primary ingredient that a great thinker needs to climb the ladder of success and remain there contentedly. Success attained by a selfish goal does not last, but that which is established and strengthened by God will stand. This does not mean you will not be faced with challenges and adversities, but you will be able to endure all things through Christ, which gives you strength. Having a winning mentality is excellent. Going after your dream is great, but having God at the forefront of your life is the greatest. Always remember that it is He that will enable you to achieve it. Now get up and do something about it!

Failure to make any attempt at progress is already a failure of mindset. Win within first, and then you can conquer what is on the outside.

Chapter 7
Against All Odds
(You Can Still Win)

"I can do all things through Christ which strengtheneth me." Phillipians: 4:13

Failure to make any attempt toward reaching your goals while casting blame on distractions and deterrents means you have successfully failed at breaking the odds and possessing a winning mentality. A lack of determination will only produce non-progressiveness and more likely find you casting blame on other things for your lack of achievement rather than yourself. After all, you are the one who did not attempt, so why expect a withdrawal when you have nothing deposited? Your lack of progress will result from your shortcomings; therefore, don't hate others when they are benefiting from their down payments. As stated earlier, serving the Lord comes with benefits; however, such service comes with sacrifice and determination. On this note, I will ask what hinders you from attaining your goal. Don't be deceived; your most significant challenge is not what you will face on the path of faith but the one within. Until you have overcome this, you will never complete the task you are determined to accomplish. Don't expect to gain divine breakthrough if you are carrying carnality with you. Therefore, mortify the flesh, that your spirit may live and ultimately access the breakthrough – when you please the Lord, He will please you.

FAULTY DOCTRINES

Faulty doctrines are another cause for many to stumble on the path of faith. One such teaching is the fast-rising prosperity message and its repeated misappropriation and misrepresentation of Biblical scriptures, which often lead some Christians to believe they are not 'prospering' because of their lack of faith and no seed sowing. These messages imply that prosperity only equates to wealth and material possessions. Those indoctrinated are convinced that not having wealth and desirable possessions, they are not prospering and see their challenges as curses.

One commonly quoted scripture used to justify their false claims comes from Philippians 4:13, "I can do all things through Christ which strengthened me." Prosperity advocates interpret this verse to mean whatever you set out to attain; you can do it, for Christ will give you the strength to do so. By this interpretation, they have implied that the Lord's arms can be twisted – for once they have willed it, He will make it possible – the same as 'name it and claim it.' I only have one question: Where is God in it if I name it and claim it? Their error is made by cementing the passage's (read Philippians 4:1-13) proper emphasis on the object of desire rather than the subject's resilience. The latter was Paul's declaration. He writes: "Not that I speak in respect of want for I have learned, in whatsoever state I am, in addition to that to be content. I know both how to be abased, and I know how to abound: everywhere and in all things, I am instructed both to be full and to be hungry, both to abound and to suffer need" (Philippians 4:11-12). What stands out from these verses is that Paul remained content and untroubled in everything. Everything here refers to every state – the good, the bad, and the ugly. The verses speak of enduring any conditions instead of attaining a goal or prize. This was Paul's premise.

In a nutshell, the Apostle stated he endured (not attained) all things through Christ, who gave him the strength to do so. This is similar to the Lord's reply to him: 'My grace is sufficient to keep you,' after Paul had asked Him to remove the thorn from his flesh on three occasions, which He denied. Instead, the Lord promised to give Paul His grace to endure.

Paul's response was quite intriguing. His words were:

"Most gladly, therefore, will I rather glory in my infirmities that the power of Christ may rest upon me. Therefore, I take pleasure in infirmities, reproaches, necessities, persecutions, distresses for Christ's sake: for when I am weak, then am I strong" (2 Corinthians 12:9-10).

To paraphrase, Paul demonstrated that he welcomed and anticipated suffering.

Proponents of this 'health and wealth gospel' would have considerable issues digesting the concept of being content during times of lack because it blatantly contradicts their more popular view. For the record, I have no qualms with prosperity. It should not be taught one-sided (ignoring the other side of the coin - long-suffering).

Seeking after goals is good; however, we all should be enlightened that obtaining them will require our endurance. Prosperity adherents should teach their followers to attain goals/success and endure the process involved, as the only way to attain this is to endure what lies ahead. Determination with endurance (hinged on Christ's strength) is the secret formula for winning.

OMAR WEDDERBURN

WITHOUT FAITH, IT IS IMPOSSIBLE TO WIN (MARK 10:48-52)

The story of Bartimaeus speaks of overpowering through any disabilities to attain the desired result. He was a blind beggar who sat by the wayside soliciting food or money. Like any other day, he was hoping to receive generous gifts from those passing by when he heard the news of Jesus passing his way (may this remind you that even with your disabilities, Jesus will still find it necessary to pass your way). Despite Bartimaeus being blind, he decided to cry out with a loud voice, 'Jesus! thou son of David, have mercy on me!' Bartimaeus' cry was not an empty one. Its Greek equivalent means to croak like a crow. The word characterizes an urgent need for attention, a vociferous cry. How comforting it is to know that God hears and saves His children when they need Him urgently.

Unlike others, Bartimaeus knew exactly what he needed and what to do, who were quick to quit at a moment's notice because of seeming limitations. What if Bartimaeus had said, "I am blind; what can I do?" Moping about situations does not assist with winning.

Here are some triumphant lessons to be learned from Bartimaeus' situation:

He was blind, but he was not deaf – The story says he heard that Jesus was passing by his way. We know that 'faith comes by hearing and hearing by the Word of God.' Bartimaeus did not see what was happening around him, but he knew that someone extraordinary was around, for he heard it from the people. Faith is just like that – to believe it (which comes by hearing), you don't have to see it.

He was blind, but he was not dumb – The story says he cried after Jesus, having heard that He was passing by his way. I am reminded of a psalm of David: "This poor man cried, and the Lord heard him. He saved him out of all his trouble." Like any good father, our Heavenly Father expects His children to cry out to Him in times of trouble, and as a good Father, He will attend to the needs of His children. Faith is just like that – it gets God's attention.

He was blind, but he was not crippled – The story says he rose/leaped up and walked to Jesus. This is reassuring because we know that the believers walk not by sight but by faith. Bartimaeus did not see Jesus, nor did he have to, as long as he knew to whom he was walking. That is just like faith – you don't have to see where you are going as long as you know to whom (Jesus) you are going.

God is supernatural and, therefore, requires faith (that which is not limited to measurement) to please Him. The

Lord is not moved, nor can He be pleased by our senses and perceptions because they are measurable variables. If our senses and perception moved God, that would make Him measurable, and if He is measurable, he cannot be infinite or sovereign. Since God is infinite, it therefore requires an immeasurable entity to please Him – that entity is faith, which, without He, can't give any acceptance.

REJECTION TO BE QUIET

Bartimaeus was told to keep quiet, but when one is desperate to win, one will never keep still. The event implies that those restraining him from crying out felt he was disrupting the procession. It's funny how some people would not see you sitting on the wayside, stuck in your dilemmas, but the moment you decide to send up praise and do something extraordinary amid the conditions, they will notice you. Bartimaeus was noticed, however, not for the right reason. He was made out to be a disruptor. Consequently, some of the men tried to restrain him. Contrary to the thought of his restrainers, Bartimaeus' 'ruption' was not a disruption but an interruption. The difference between the two is that the former causes mayhem and the latter causes cessation. When Bartimaeus cried out, Jesus and the crowd that followed him paused.

Perhaps when the children of God cry out (by faith), they are interrupting heaven? Could it be that when the church begins to praise and worship (through faith) their Heavenly Father, there is an urgency in heaven to act on their behalf?

> Psalm 22:3 comes close to implicating this: "But thou art holy, o thou that inhabitest the praises of Israel."

Interestingly, the word inhabits here means to dwell, remain, sit, and abide. The projection is that God sits, abides, and remains with them whenever Israel offers her praise alongside faith. Even more interesting, a primitive root of the word means to crouch, specifically in the posture of an ambush. How refreshing is knowing that my worship, praise, and faith create an ambush in the spiritual?

We remember King Jehoshaphat, whom the Lord instructed to go out against his enemies with praise. Have we forgotten what happened to Israel's enemies when they glorified the Lord? I will remind you that 'the Lord set an ambush' against the enemies of Israel (Read 2 Chronicles 20:22).

So, whatever odds you face, be assured that faith, prayer, and worship are the ambushments that ultimately lead to a breakthrough.

So, while the believer's faith interrupts heaven, the kingdom of darkness, on the other hand, experiences mayhem.

The grand lesson from Bartimaeus' actions is that there ought not to be any situations in your life dark enough to inhibit your worship, stop you from hearing God's words, or hinder your walk with God. As Bartimaeus relied on his available strengths, do not let shortcomings distract you from your available strengths.

YOU MUST CONSTANTLY PRAY TO WIN (1 KINGS 18:41-44)

Elijah was a man like we are. He prayed earnestly that it would not rain, and it did not for three and a half years. Elijah's prayer validates the scripture: "The prayer of a righteous person is powerful and effective" (James 5:16). So, what makes prayer powerful and effective? Simply, it is the prayer of a righteous individual. Behind an effective and powerful prayer is an effective and powerful pray-er (the one who prays). I often compare a powerful, effective prayer to a holy, acceptable sacrifice. If the sacrifice doesn't meet the ceremonial requirements, the Lord will not accept it. Likewise, a pray-er that doesn't meet holy standards will be ineffective. Never has an altar gone to the sacrifice; it is always the sacrifice that is brought to the altar. Do not expect God's approval if you are unwilling to sacrifice. Can you identify any unacceptable things that must be put to death for your Heavenly Father to approve of you?

Therefore, you must not pray only when you desire to but pray because your Heavenly Father desires you to. What father does not want his children to desire him?

After defeating Jezebel's prophets on Mount Carmel, Elijah said he heard an abundance of rain. After which, he went further up the mountain to pray. Should he not be more concerned about the impending showers than going up to pray? It is always good to hear a word in your spirit, but it is better and wise to always pray about it. That is precisely what Elijah went to do. Seven times, he prayed, and at each interval, he asked his servant to look toward the sea's horizon to see if there was a climatic change, but each time, the servant would bring a bad report. Yet, Elijah continued to pray. Likewise, God desires His children to pray consistently, even when they do not see a change. The word of God says, "Pray without ceasing." Consistent praying will 'open heaven.'

When you are convicted of what you have heard from the Spirit, you will pray until you see what you have heard.

On the seventh attempt, the servant saw a cloud the size of a man's hand. He went back to Elijah, obviously disappointed - his manner of reporting was a testament to that fact. He said all I see is 'a cloud the size of a man's hand.' He could not comprehend his master's hearing of an abundance of rain with him seeing a small cloud. Many Christians are like this. They complain when the word does not meet their expectations. Usually, when God says something and what you see appears contrary, He is up to something abundant. That is how complainers easily miss a divine opportunity because of its appearance. Elijah's servant mistakenly concluded that the cloud's size was too small to bring abundant rain. The real problem was not the size of the cloud but his distance away from the cloud.

He would have understood if he had spent time observing the cloud rather than complaining about its size. Refrain from making the same mistake as this servant; you might not get another chance. The ball is in your court to be either a complainer or a prayer warrior.

TO WIN, DON'T LOSE HOPE (2 KINGS 7:1-11)

Every Christian will face uphill challenges, which should not come as a surprise as 'many are the afflictions of the righteous.' Christianity's road is the best path for one to take, but it is not without roadblocks and delays, primarily engineered and conducted by Christendom's leading flagman – the devil! In my 24 years of ministry, I have not met one believer who has never encountered his path. Sadly, too, I met others who got weary of the delays and subsequently detoured from the way.

I have come to learn that hopelessness and disappointment make it easy for the devil to manipulate the believers.

If you are continuously disappointed, either the Lord wants you to learn something from the experiences, or you are too proud to acknowledge that your actions are not working. Why not do it God's way instead of your way? But for many people, including some Christians, God's way is the long way. I'd rather trust God and do it His way than the 'easy' way that will likely cost me a lifetime of regret. Our Heavenly Father wants us to cast our cares unto Him. He should be our foremost resort in everything we do. The Psalmist asserts, 'In Him will I trust.' So why lose hope when Father is the creator of all things? As I ponder on the Father's abundant care for His children, I recall the story of the four lepers (I previously mentioned them in Chapter 6), who delivered Israel from what appeared to be a hopeless situation. But the four men themselves, by their physical conditions, were more affected. The story's backdrop presents the city of Samaria and its people starving from a dreadful famine. Food was so scarce that people, including children, started eating what they would not have typically eaten. To make matters worse, the people were surrounded by their enemies, the Syrians. So, venturing outside the city's wall in search of food was not an option. Until one day, a message of hope came from the most unlikely source – four leprous men who sat outside the city's main gate.

Unlike those within the city walls, the four were exposed to any enemy attack. Starving and without any protection, it seemed their best option was to prepare to die. But one of the four had an idea. It was a "nothing to lose" idea. He encouraged his other friends to give themselves to the Syrians, who were camping far away. "Why sit here and wait until we die? Let's give ourselves over to the Syrians. Chances are they might spare our lives, but if they do not, we are dead men either way, so what is there to lose?" In the night, the four started their journey. It turned out that the Lord would use their hopeful decision to change the outcome of a nation. As they journeyed toward the Syrian camp, the Lord amplified their feet so that the Syrians heard what sounded like an army coming against them. In haste, every man fled, leaving his valuables and possessions. When the four got to the camp, it was empty and all for the taking. They ate and drank and also hid gold and silver for themselves. But what they did next is worthy of commendation. They decided to return to their city and tell the king about their findings. Eventually, a small contingent of the king's servants returned food to the people.

It was a beautiful ending that would not have happened if these four men had not made what I call a "hopeful decision" to move out.

SIX OBSERVATIONS

1. Complaining won't change your situation; adjustment (movement made to achieve a desired result) will. If some people spent as much time and energy on making adjustments as they did complaining about their situations, their lives would be much better. Don't waste time talking about how hopeless it is. Instead, use your time wisely to create hopeful ideas.
2. Scourged men with faith are better than whole men with fear.
3. Hope is not prejudiced. By this, I mean you don't have to be 'whole' to embrace it. Stop pinning hopelessness on your condition because it doesn't appear how you would like it to.
4. Ceremonially, the four were unclean men, but their conditions did not deter them from making a move of faith. Are you considering making a faith move but fearing it will yield nothing? What is there to lose? You might be surprised at what is waiting out there for you.

5. Steps of faith terrify the ear of the enemy. The faithful will overcome Satan with their word and testimonies. It is Satan's desire for you to be dormant and lack faith. Faith is your defense, like a shield; you are left open to his fiery darts without it. That serpent is terrified by faith; he hates hearing the saints declaring God's name. Having your faith anchored on the work and word of Jesus Christ, you are bound to win. God will grant His provisions from the most unlikely source to sustain His children. God provided the ravens to feed Elijah, a large fish to prevent Jonah from drowning, a ram caught in a thicket for Abraham's sacrifice, and spoils from the Syrian camp to feed a hungry nation, so what reason is there to be hopeless?

6. When God blesses you, be a blessing to others in return. When God blesses you, do not be mean with it; go and bless others. A brother or sister is praying faithfully for a breakthrough and hoping for a blessing. You may be the answer to his or her prayer. Hope must not just be desired; it also must be shared.

TO WIN, YOU MUST BREAK THE RULES
(COLOSSIANS 2:8)

This, by no stretch of the imagination, encourages rebellion. On the contrary, this urges revolution. Sometimes, to have positive impacts, rules that keep one bound have to be broken, particularly man-made rules. Rules are necessary for keeping order, as the Apostles established rules in the early church. However, the rules they instituted were for moral and ethical guidance within the body of Christ, not laws established to bind and control the saints under a man-made system. Salvation is liberty, not bondage. Anything that cannot be substantiated with the word of God is bondage. To be set free, you must release yourself from man-made rules and submit to God-made rules. The Apostle Paul puts it like this, "Beware lest any man spoil (take you captive) through philosophy and vain deceit, after the tradition of men, after the rudiments of the world, and not after Christ" (Colossians 2:8). I realize that many saints have missed their opportunity to soar because they have been bound to a system established by man and not God. Many church leaders have set rules to elevate themselves rather than God; they build empires rather than God's Kingdom. They set rules to keep you in fear of them rather than God. To win, you must come from among them.

Don't be deceived. Your greatest challenge is not what you will face on the path of faith, but the one that is within. Until determined to win, the probability of successfully completing the task is marginally slim.

Chapter 8
"A Desperate Tear"

"And when they could not come nigh unto Him for the press, they uncovered the roof where He was: and when they had broken it up, they let down the bed wherein the sick of the palsy laid." Mark 2:4

It is often said that a 'drowning man will clutch at a straw' or 'desperate times call for desperate measures.' These two expressions are a perfect description of the men in this story.

The account is about a man who was sick with palsy (paralyzed or had a stroke). He was brought by his four friends, who heard Jesus was in their region and decided to seek Him out to heal their friend. When they got to the site where Jesus was, all doors were blocked by the present thick crowd. Have you ever had a dire need that required urgent attention, but all the available entrances are blocked? What do you do then? Do you abandon the mission because of the obstacles? Do you complain or do something about it? Faith is not about doing nothing but actively trusting the Lord's promises amid setbacks. So, what are you going to do about your situation? Here is something to note: Faith is not an act but an actuality. This means that it is not the action that determines the result but the predetermined result that inspires the action. Therefore, a walk by faith is knowing that the result is already done - not wishing for it to be done. Faith is more of evidence and less of an expectation, even though the evidence incites the expectation.

GIFT OF DESPERATION

The scene (Mark 2:1-12) describes a situation where desperate men brought their paralyzed friend on a bed to a crowded place so he could be healed. However, upon their arrival, the location was inaccessible due to the large crowd there. The friend on the bed made it even more difficult for them to press through the crowd; therefore, the four men looked for another entrance. The five men decided they were going to do something about the situation. They resolved on a radical act - to tear a part of the roof of the house to get into Jesus' presence. Unlike others who had settled with being on the outside, these men were desperate to get inside.

This desperation indicates that the men understood Jesus' ministry and had faith enough to take action. Arguably, the men must have calculated the risks, counted the cost, and consciously decided that their friend would be healed, whatever it took. They must have analysed Jesus' ministry and considered the primary signs of His presence.

SIGNS

These signs included a crowd – A crowd always followed Jesus, even when He tried to sneak into a region. His presence always attracted a gathering that often included people in need of a breakthrough, in need of healing, and needing to know Him. But there were others among the crowd that had ulterior intentions, namely the Pharisees and Sadducees, who only gathered to seek ways to accuse and kill Jesus. A second sign that accompanied Jesus' presence was signs and wonders. Thirdly, Jesus' presence was announced by noise (proclamation, buzz).

Since these three occurrences were common with Jesus' ministry and presence, does this mean if one's local church is missing these phenomena, it could be that His presence is not there? Something for you to ponder.

It is obvious that the men knew the signs and were clear about their objectives. Here are three things worth mentioning about them:

There was a preconceived decision not to be spectators. They aimed to get into the house where Jesus was. They did not open the roof to have a view of what was happening on the inside. They wanted more than just to hear Jesus or to see him, they needed a miracle for their friend. Standing outside or being in the crowd would get them nowhere.

MAKE IT HAPPEN

They had to leave the comfort of being followers and do something unorthodox for the desired result. Sadly, too many spectators are in churches today. They are waiting for something to happen rather than making something happen. It seems that Christians have forgotten the old story told about the children of Israel and the manna from God. God fed Israel with manna but did not allow it to fall in their camps. Instead, the manna fell on the outskirts. Israel had to go and gather the food and bring it back to their camps. Stop sitting around waiting for provisions to fall out of thin air and get your daily needs. Desperate people go after manna and tear roofs to meet their needs.

They had to tear a hole big enough. The four men let down their sick friend when the hole was the correct size. Making a hole was not enough for them; they had to ensure the final dimensions were perfect to comfortably fit through their friend's bed. In other words, you must calculate and evaluate your situation before making a desperate tear. One of the reasons so many Christians have not received their breakthrough already is because the hole being torn is not big enough. We have been trying to force ourselves into holes we have not measured sufficiently. Quit trying to squeeze yourself through tiny holes. Please measure your situation first. Be familiar with it so you will know how big a tear you need and how desperate you are to make this attempt count. Therefore, a calculated risk is essential to your deliverance. Will you tear open heaven for your breakthrough? A wise statement of the ages declares that only fools rush in without evaluations. Without evaluations, you are bound to fail. You are expected, at least, to assess the situation considering that this could be your only attempt. Another noteworthy consideration is to cease blaming others when things are unplanned. A blockage is not necessarily a deterrent; it could be a test for the glorification of God's holy name. Rather than complain about the crowd blocking the entrance, the men strategize another route.

They knew exactly where to lower the sick man. It was not enough to lower their friend into the room; they aimed to lower him precisely in front of Jesus. Doing it this way, there was no way Jesus could have missed him. When was the last time you lowered your situation at the feet of Jesus, even as these men lowered theirs before Him? The lowering here serves as a symbol of humility and worship. Humility and worship will get you noticed by God. The text says that Jesus noticed their faith. 'Their faith' also included the man sick with palsy. Though he was the one paralyzed, Jesus saw his faith also. Having a 'paralyzed' situation is no excuse to lose faith. I believe the paralyzed man influenced and initiated his friends to act on his behalf. How so? Well, because he was the one with the condition. Therefore, it is likely that he was the one giving the orders. The paralyzed man's faith was beyond his condition. Jesus, seeing his faith, said to the sick, 'Your sins are forgiven.' How disappointed he must have been hearing these words from Jesus. After all, he did not go through the ordeal only to be told that his sins were forgiven - he needed healing, too. Let me explain why Jesus did this. The cultural mindset of the people was that a physical ailment was a result of past sins. Perhaps this man had been living with the guilt that his condition was a result of his past, so Jesus comforted him by not only healing his physical condition but also his spiritual condition. Also present at this grand staging of faith and miracles were the Pharisees. The view was that a man's condition was linked to his sinful past. If Jesus had healed the man without dealing with his sins, the Pharisees would have challenged Jesus because the healing was not of God. Jesus ensured that the Pharisees had no doubt or accusation.

LEAVE DIFFERENTLY

Jesus then told the paralyzed man to take up his bed and go. The bed was symbolic of where and what he used to be. The thing that once held him, he now holds it; the thing which once managed him, he was managing it; the thing that once controlled him, he is controlling it. Jesus could have told him to rise and go but telling him to take up his bed is a sign of total deliverance.

In other words, the situation that once held you captive and prevented your freedom, you will now hold that situation in your hand as a testimony. Let's remember the words of these verses from the Psalms: "You have given me the necks of my enemies" (Psalm 18:40) And "You teacheth my hands to war and my fingers to fight" (Psalm 144:1). Therefore you, too, can praise God for His goodness toward you. He can give you your 'bed' to carry for a testimony.

The paralyzed man came in through the roof, but he walked out the door. What does this mean? He did not leave the way he came in. He came in through the roof, paralyzed, and went through the door walking. You will not leave the same way you came in after making a desperate tear and lowering yourself in humility. "This poor man cried, and the Lord heard him and delivered him out of his troubles" (Psalm 34:6). The believers worship symbolically rip heaven open and lower them before God. If you are desperate for deliverance, use that desperation to tear heaven's roof.

Desperate times call for desperate measures. Don't allow adversities or setbacks to block you from deliverance. How desperately do you need it?

CHAPTER 9
I WILL NOT BE WEARIED

"For His anger endureth but a moment, in His favor is life: weeping may endure for a night, but joy cometh in the morning." Psalm 30:5

Psalm 30 is one of my favourite of David's. In this Psalm, he writes about being vulnerable yet possessing a determined drive to stay afloat amid his drowning problems by offering thanksgiving unto the Lord. Interestingly, David's thanksgiving came before he cried for help unto the Lord: "O Lord my God, I cried unto thee, and thou hast healed me." Unlike so many others, David could have gotten distracted by his problem and complained about it to God but instead offered thanksgiving first. You, like David, must recognize that praise sets precedence over problems. To be thankful to the Lord in the midst of problems is to surrender them into His hands.

TIME TO CELEBRATE

Therefore, be encouraged that you don't have to wait until you are physically out of the muddle to start celebrating your breakthrough.

Having set the precedence, David then exhorts the saints to worship, reassuring them that the crisis is just for a period. They will have to endure the weeping for a while, but rejoicing will eventually come to the faithful. The picture being painted here is that of a guest lodging for the night. As a result, the guest has caused severe inconvenience, leaving the host eagerly anticipating his guest leaving in the morning.

Is an unwelcome thing lodging in your life, causing you to weep? It is time to dislodge it and not spend another night in misery. Your joy will come in the morning, and because joy is inevitable, you do not have to wait until daylight to start the praising.

One of the things I like about worship is that once done in truth, it causes reflection. Have you ever started praising God for a specific thing and just thanked Him for everything He had done? This should not be a surprise, as praise is thanksgiving unto the Lord.

THE JOURNEY

Christianity is a journey; like all journeys, one must be prepared for whatever obstacles lie ahead. However, you can take comfort in that your personal Guide is the Holy Spirit. While the voyage will not be hassle-free, the Guide will guarantee your safe arrival to the destination. You aim to complete the task and have absolute confidence in His direction. You don't always see or know what the Lord is doing, yet you faithfully follow Him. Why is this so? Because you know that once He is leading you, everything will be alright. Psalm 23:2 writes: "He leadeth me beside the still waters." Note the verse did not say running waters. The Lord knew the current would have driven the sheep downstream, so He led the animal to where it was safe – still waters! Since the Lord is always leading you to a safe place, your obedience, trust, and patience are needed: "For yea though I walk through the valley of the shadow of death I will fear no evil for thou art with me, thy rod and thy staff they comfort me." The Lord's protection and guidance are sure; He will lead you through the 'shadows.' Therefore, He can more than lead you through the object that is casting the shadow. With such comfort and assurance, you can be wary of predicaments but not be weary of them.

YOU WILL REAP

The Apostle Paul wrote to the churches at Galatia: "Be not weary in doing well, for you shall REAP in due season if you faint not." The word REAP means to harvest (in the sense of crop). It pictures a planter who goes out to sow. However, he does not begin to sow with the expectation to reap immediately after, as he already knows the reaping will require several processes and his patience. The undertakings of reaping can be tumultuous, but his expectation of harvest drives the planter – it is what keeps him motivated – he anticipates the time of reaping from all his hard work.

Paul likens this to the Christian's journey, filled with obstacles. He encourages the saints not to get weary but to work with the expectation that they will reap in due season. Paul's sentiment inspires all Christians not to be discombobulated by the distractions, disappointments, and hardships coming at them. Regardless, Christians should still keep their heads up high. For, after all, we are still here – we have not given up.

Though forsaken by family and friends, trouble from all sides, weapons formed against you, mocked, ridiculed, scorned, confused, and do not know what to do next, you must not be disconcerted but take encouragement from the

Lord's word that He 'will not leave nor forsake you.' It is a promise He must keep, as He cannot lie. Therefore, be resolute, as Job declared,

> "Naked I came into this world and naked I shall return, the Lord gives, and the Lord takes away, but blessed is the name of the Lord. You turn my wailing into dancing; you remove my sackcloth and clothed me with joy, that my heart may sing to You and not be silent. O Lord my God, I will give you thanks forever."

The Lord's comfort and assurance are a guarantee; you need not worry, but keep striving and striding, for you will reap the harvest from the labour you have endured – your joy will gladly come in the morning.

Knowing that what lies ahead is much greater than what you are facing now is ultimately all the encouragement you need to complete the journey. In the end, it will be better.

CHAPTER 10
LIVING ON THE EDGE

"But put forth thine hand now, and touch all that he hath, and he will curse you to your face." "Hath not thou made a hedge about him, and about his house, and about all that he hath on every side? Thou hast blessed the work of his hands, and his substance is increased in the land." Job 1:10-11

Why does an all-powerful and good God allow bad things to happen to good people? Why do Christians suffer? Is God just? Does He exist? These are frequently asked by Christians who have experienced suffering or are encountering adversity. Sometimes, their thought of hope is as discouraging as the trial itself because God appears to be silent or absent. However, regardless, the faithful Christians remain unmoved. Why is this so? Embedded in the faithful saints' spirits is the hope that their sovereign Lord and just Creator will deliver them from suffering. So, in all honesty, the believers should not question God's existence nor His justice but instead ask themselves, 'How faithful am I?'

Can you still trust God when things around you are erratic and contrary to His word? Job's story reflects a man whose relationship with God was unaffected, regardless of the afflictions he encountered. Job was respected by God and regarded by Him as a man of faithfulness and righteousness. The scripture states: "There was no one on earth like him; he was blameless and upright, a man who fears God and shuns evil" (Job 1:8 & 2:3).

FAITH OR THEODICY

Some theologians believe that the general theme of Job is Theodicy. Theodicy attempts to defend and articulate the justice of God in light of human suffering and evil, especially that of the innocent and righteous. Its primary purpose seeks to dispel the assumptions that God is not just and does not exist. But long before theodicy was considered a theological discipline, God's people (Israel) already believed in His justice and existence. Thus, the Jews' conclusion of suffering is that it was indicative of one's sins. This was the precise claim made against Job by his friends, who initially heard of his demise and came to encourage him. But after seeing his state, all three men concluded that

Job's affliction was the result of an offense he committed. They identified Job's condition to be a curse and justified. Don't be quick to make hasty conclusions, as these three men did. Perception is not reality!

GOD INITIATED THE TEST

It is interesting or strange, depending on how you look at it, that God decided to allow Satan to afflict Job shortly after He had lauded him for his righteousness before the same accuser. I believe God allows the accuser to press the believers to bring out the best in them. Yes, I know it is cliche, but it is the truth. Grapes don't become wine until they have been pressed. What is often perceived as a curse could be a blessing in disguise, as proven later in Job's life.

The story unfolds with a meeting in Heaven, where Satan presents himself. God asks him, 'Where have you come from?' Satan replies, 'From walking up and down in the earth.' Then suddenly, God asks another question unrelated to the previous, "Have you considered my servant Job?" Why did God ask this question? Isn't He all-knowing? Well, the question was rhetorical. God wanted the devil to acknowledge His tribute to Job and that He was aware of his intention - to accuse Job. The Hebrew word for Satan means accuser; therefore, Satan's sole purpose in presenting himself was to do likewise. However, before Satan could say a word against Job, God validated him as a righteous and faithful man. When a saint's faith is authentic, it discredits Satan's accusation - he can make a claim, but it will not be valid.

As stated earlier, God initiated the dialogue that led to Job's suffering and His subsequent permission to afflict Job. Considering that Job was a just servant, why did the Lord allow this? Some people find it unsettling to accept that God permits suffering as much as He prevents it.

FROM TEST TO TESTAMENT

The affliction of the saints is a testament to their relationship with God. An analogy I learned and often illustrates puts it like this: Christianity is a journey, to which if you have not met the devil face to face, you are both heading in the same direction. Satan's opposition to the saints indicates they are not walking in his direction. Thus, the saints' inadvertent affliction.

"For in this you greatly rejoice though now for a little while you may have suffered grief in all kinds of trials. These have come so that your faith – of greater worth than gold, which perishes even though refined by fire -- may be proved genuine and may result in praise, glory, and honour when

Jesus Christ is revealed" (1 Peter 1:6). In the above passage, Peter presents his audience with two objects: fire and gold. The Apostle's primary emphasis was gold, as it was the element that changed from impurity to purity. The fire, on the other hand, remained constant. Figuratively, gold represents the saints, and the fire represents trial. Peter told the saints to remain faithful amid trial because it would improve them. Sounds easier said than done, right? But seriously, is the walk of faith an easy path? Honestly, most, if not all, Christians will respond with a resounding no. Therefore, we depend on the Holy Spirit's guidance and strength to bring us through. With the Holy Spirit's aid, we are assured of safe arrival to our destination, regardless of the bumps.

Job, the faithful servant of the Lord, was placed into the fire, not by Satan but by the Lord Himself, since He was the initiator. Yet, Job did not deny or curse God - faithfully remained on the edge. Have you ever been on the edge? Maybe you are on one now. 'On the edge' denotes a precarious position, i.e., hopelessness and despair.

It is Satan's desire for Christians to go off the edge. So be sober and alert, for he is a roaming and roaring lion seeking whom he may devour.

SATAN'S THREE-FOLD PLOT

Satan's accusation against Job was that he was only faithful because the Lord had placed a hedge around him, but if God should remove the hedge, Job would curse Him. Then, shockingly, God permitted Satan to afflict Job in all areas except his soul. From that moment, Satan launched his threefold plot to destroy Job.

Firstly, he orchestrated the removal of the hedge around Job (it was the shield keeping him from going off the edge). Having successfully gotten the hedge to be removed, Satan's second attempt was to shove Job off the edge. His third strategy was to find himself an accomplice - Job's wife. Yes, you better believe it! She was an unaware abetter. Remember that this was not the serpent's first scheming attempt - he beguiled Eve in the Garden of Eden into the fall of Adam. Job's wife, in an emotional attempt to comfort her husband from misery, said to him, "Are you still maintaining your integrity? Curse God and die!" (Job 2:9). Please note how her last four words were the same as Satan said Job would do. This strengthens the point that she was an unaware participant of Satan's scheme. Fortunately, Job did not fall for the trap and rebuked his wife's attempt, calling it a 'foolish' one. Throughout the affliction, Job did not sin in charging God with wrongdoing. With words like "naked I came from my mother's womb and naked will I depart, the Lord gave, and the Lord has taken away, may the name of the Lord be praised" (Job 1:21-22) as a testament to his faithfulness. Essentially, Job was making it known that his possession was given to him by the Lord, and if it pleases the Lord to take them away, it does not change His existence or justice.

STAND YOUR GROUND

Christians are on the edge when hopeless situations arise. Sometimes, it feels like the only thing to do is to take a last breath and plunge. This is precisely what Satan wants the believers to do – commit a spiritual suicide. But like Job, the believers must remain resilient and defiant. The Psalmist reminds us, "Weeping may endure for a night, but joy is coming in the morning… for a brief moment He abandons you, but with deep compassion, He will bring you back" (Psalm 30:5, Isaiah 54:7). The believer that endures the ills of the night will be joyful in the morning.

Job was on the edge but refused to lose faith in the Lord - instead, he worshipped. Do not cease to worship the Lord because your life isn't adding up. Remember, if he did it before, He can do it again.

Job cursed the day he was born but never went off the edge. In all his appointed time, he waited until his change came. "Though He slays me, yet will I hope in Him, I will surely defend my ways to His face." (Job 13:15). Job believed he would be vindicated. His patience in the light of his suffering reflected his discipline and tenacity. In the end, he received double for his trouble. His experience is a lesson for all Christians to learn to trust God in suffering and see its great reward.

What seemed like being at the edge of a breakdown was the edge of a breakthrough. Losing is not an indicator that you have lost.

Don't be deceived. Not all stripping is the result of a mess up – some is clearly a set up.

What appears to be an edge of despair could actually be your edge of a breakthrough.

CHAPTER 11
THEN SUDDENLY

"And suddenly there was a great earthquake so that the foundations of the prison were shaken: and immediately all the doors were opened, and every one's bands were loosed." Acts 16:26

There will come moments when the Lord will do something unexpected that surprises His children. We can never calculate His next move. He is not a formula that the most outstanding mathematicians can solve. He does things that have you expressing, 'Hmmm!'

IDENTIFY THE SOURCE

One day, Paul and his companion Silas were heading out to pray when a young girl with a fortune-telling spirit met them. Her masters had made a fortune off her 'telling.' This young girl followed Paul and Silas for many days, crying out, "'These men are the servants of the most high God, which show us the way of salvation." The demon spirit, the source of her gift, knew who Paul and Silas were (don't be so intrigued by gifted people that you are unaware of the source of their gifts). Not every gift is Godly. Satan is gifted too

Evil spirits know who the children of God are. There was once a man possessed with a 'legion' (many) of demons. When he saw Jesus, the demons in him cried, saying, "Let us alone, what have we to do with thee, thou Jesus of Nazareth? Art, thou come to destroy us? I know thee who thou art, the Holy One of God." Notice the demons said they knew who Jesus was. Evil spirits will see the reflection of the Father on the believers; their Father's light will radiate from them.

After several days of continuous 'telling,' Paul was annoyed and commanded the spirit to come out of her. When her masters, to whom she had brought much wealth, saw that the source of their gain was no more, they were angry and seized Paul and Silas and took them to the magistrates. How sad it is that there are selfish people in the world, thinking about themselves while disregarding the well-being of others. The young girl was abused by her masters to make themselves wealthy - their ill-treatment of her was not a concern as long as she was making money for them.

Perhaps you have met some people like this young girl's masters. They will never be happy for your breakthrough but their own.

LOCKED UP

Paul and Silas were eventually brought to the magistrates and found guilty, beaten, and thrown into prison. The two men were incarcerated for setting a young girl free and preaching the gospel. From all accounts, their actions were noble, yet they were sent to prison for being good men. In this crazy world, ungodliness has more company and popularity than righteousness. Why? Because their lord (the devil) has blinded their eyes. As a Christian living in a world where its ruler is the father of immortality, you must embrace the reality that your good works and words will not always be received with joy. As a result of this, many Christians have shunned their faith openly for the sake of being men-pleasers. If you are being prosecuted for proclaiming the truth of God, consider it a privilege. One of Christendom's problems is that many saints fear being persecuted, so they conform to the worldly system. Be encouraged; the Lord will not leave nor forsake His children. Fear not the man that can kill the body alone but the One who has power over both body and spirit. If doing the right thing will cause others to hate you, let them hate. This should not surprise the saints, for Jesus had given the disciples (and, by extension, the church) a heads-up of this reality. He said, "If the world hates you, you know it hated me before it hated you. If ye were of the world, the world would love its own: but because ye are not of the world, but I have chosen you out of the world, therefore the world hateth you" (John 15:18). Be bold about your faith; stand for holiness, without fear or excuse. There is no excuse for being holy. The last time I checked the Bible, holiness was the standard God required.

BOUND BUT STILL PRAISING

Paul and Silas were sent to prison for doing the right thing. But while they were there, at midnight, they began to praise God. You learned to still praise God during 'midnight' moments and 'prison' positions.

Along with Paul and Silas were other prisoners equally bound. However, regardless of their plight, they heard (listened to) Paul and Silas' praise. The verb implies that they were partaking in the worship. Paul and Silas were fastened (locked, tied) to shackles in prison, but that did not hinder them from praying and praising. But while they were praising, the other prisoners acknowledged and listened intently, though they were in the same predicament. They weren't too tied up to acknowledge praise. If the prisoners in their position could recognize and listen, there should be no excuse for you to be tied up from giving God what belongs to Him.

The enemy desires to keep you bound, and you focus on your conditions rather than on God. How often have you said I am too 'tied up' to give God the time He deserves? Can you stop focusing on the issues at hand and give Him praise? The expression 'tied up' is a figure of speech for being busy or occupied with something that, subsequently, exhibits the individual's disregard for other things. Ignoring moments to pray and praise because you are 'shackled' isn't an excuse not to give God what He is worth!

PRISON BREAK

As they sang praises during their predicament, a SUDDEN earthquake shook the foundation of the prison, and all the prisoners' bands fell free. When things don't seem to be looking up, don't be discouraged, but still trust the Lord in His words.

Your faithfulness to the Lord will be rewarded. Not everyone in front of you is ahead of you, and not everyone ahead of you is genuinely better than you. Only some people ahead accessed their achievements by pure means. When the saints delight the Lord, He will give His blessings. He may give you a fast-track breakthrough - swift and sudden. So, keep praising and praying without ceasing, even in destitute places and conditions.

The Lord has a way of showing up big when you least expect it. He is great and there is no predicament too vast for Him to "shake" and "release" you from.

On that note, always anticipate a sudden breakthrough.

CHAPTER 12
THERE IS A CAUSE

"Therefore, my beloved brethren, be ye steadfast, unmovable, always abounding the work of the Lord, forasmuch as ye know that your labor is not in vain in the Lord." (1 Corinthians 15:58)

Work smart and not hard," the voice of a woman of God constantly resounds through the years of my Christian life. This saying reminds me of what Paul was saying in the aforementioned letter to the Corinthians. You can work extra hard at the same thing for years with no results simply because you do not work smart. Working smart means applying discretion and wisdom to situations (Proverbs 2:11, Matthew 10:16). You will remain unmovable and always abounding in the work of the Lord when you apply your heart to know wisdom and understanding in your most trying situations.

The word of God says, 'No temptation has taken you except what is common to man.' Other people are experiencing worse than you at this moment. That is why your trials must not sidetrack you, as they will turn for the glory of God and work for your good. These experiences are the testaments of His grace and prove that you are closer to a breakthrough (Revelations 12:11, Romans 8:28).

Let's say hypothetically, you were setting up a significant project but then encountered a massive setback. Due to the setback, it appeared the project might not come to fruition, so you considered aborting the plan, thinking you had failed.

Unfortunately, many have made hasty decisions to quit at the slightest hint of a problem. But what if there were a light at the end of the tunnel? They might be walking away from their breakthrough. Paul explicitly states: "Don't be weary in doing well, in your due season, you shall reap if you faint not" (Galatians 6:9). The faithful saints will reap in due season because they refuse to quit (faint). However, it should be noted that the season will change; likewise, the saint must be mentally prepared for inevitable cycles. Like the seasons, cycles have a set time 'that all things work together for good to those that love God and are called according to his purpose' (Romans 8:28). Solomon concurs:

"That which hath is now, and that which is to have already been, and God requireth the things that are past" (Ecclesiastes 3:15). So, as you have read, cycle/process is important because it is specifically designed to prepare the saints and produce their purpose. Hence, it is very important to stay focused on His will.

As a result of Jesus' resurrection, serving Him is not empty – the saints' labour is not in vain. Do not hesitate to do good because the result you are looking for is not showing, but remember your effort is invested in His winning cause, always remembering and believing that 'faith is the substance of things hoped for, the evidence of things not seen' (Hebrews 11: 1). You won't often see the good results from your efforts, but it doesn't mean they aren't apparent. So, keep doing the good you have an opportunity to do, knowing that God's word will have eternal results, just as the Psalmist says, "They that sow in tears will reap in joy" (Psalm 126:5 KJV).

YOUR LABOR IS NOT IN VAIN

The Greek word used by Paul for labour is Kopos. It means a beating of the breast with grief, sorrow, and intense labour united with trouble and toil. Are you pondering giving up because of intense trouble and toil bombarding you from every end? Have you ever asked yourself, "Why do I bother?" A pregnant woman, on the day of her delivery, doesn't ask herself, why bother giving birth? She will not get up and walk out of the delivery room. On the contrary, she is well aware that delivering her child requires her labouring, and as painful as the process will be, she knows it will not be in vain. Isaiah declares, "For as soon as Zion travails, she brought forth her children" (Isaiah 66:8). Note the time when Zion gave birth to her children - as soon as she travails (a painful and laborious effort). Here, the prophet compares the trying of the saint's faith to a woman in labour about to give birth, but as soon as she delivers, she forgets the ordeal. The lesson to the saints is quite simple – birth comes after the travailing - and blessings come after the afflictions.

IF YOU FAINT, YOU WON'T REAP

Travailing, labour, and toiling are not necessarily bad things but can be signs of an impending breakthrough. Hence, it is essential to push against the turmoil because, after the worthy pain and agony, you will see a great result. Remain immovable and always abounding to the Rock (Jesus Christ) until the vision becomes a reality. Being cemented on the Rock is the core factor that will keep you grounded amid adverse elements. The wind will blow, the water will rise, and the rain will pour against you, but your feet will be planted on the solid foundation of the Rock that will determine your victory.

In Matthew 7, Jesus spoke to His disciples about judgment, bearing fruits, and how to access the kingdom. Then, in verse 24, Jesus said, "…whosoever heareth these sayings of mine and doeth them, I will liken them unto a wise man, which built his house upon a rock…" This proves that if you faint, you will not reap. If you remain wise and understand your seasons, i.e., God's plans for your life, you will appreciate the pain that comes with the purpose.

Reaping a great harvest lies in sowing good seeds while you labour. Sowing the best seeds will eventually guarantee you reap the best harvest. Paul writes, "Be not deceived God is not mocked: for whatsoever a man soweth, that shall he also reap" (Galatians 6:7). The verse shows that the saints' desired harvest is tied to their seeds sown in the process.

Having endured the labour, the saints can testify like Paul, "I have fought a good fight, I have finished my course, I have kept the faith" (2 Timothy 4:7). The word "fight" identifies a contest for victory or mastery as was used in the Greek games. Figuratively, it means to strain every nerve to the utmost toward one's goal. Here Paul was reminiscing over 30 years of his apostolic labour and announcing his victory cry like a proud athlete who had engaged successfully in a contest. Imagine a group of gladiators battling it out in an arena. The battle is heated, and each gladiator knows that even though they are a spectacle, it is a battle for survival. It is either die or fight for survival. The fight is for a cause!

Daily, the saints fight against the enemy of their salvation – a persistent opponent whose only assignment is to take them out. In their daily walk, the saints must acknowledge themselves as gladiators fighting an evangelical contest. The saints are assured of their inevitable victory through Jesus' work at Calvary.

However, they are required to guard themselves against the wiles and devices of Satan, having faith as their shield and being equipped with the armour of God. The wise man stated, "Keep thy heart with all diligence, for out of it are the issues of life" (Proverbs 4:23).

The devil's artillery of distraction can only be utilized on the battlefield of the mind. Being fully aware, Peter posits that the saints should be sober and vigilant 'because your adversary the devil walks about as a roaring lion seeking whom he may devour' (1 Peter 5: 8). Further inspection shows that the devil is not a lion, he only behaves like one - he intends to create fear. When fear is present, faith is absent.

Another note worth mentioning is that the 'whom he may' is a conditional clause - Satan's tactics are only successful on those who allow them. Satan is looking for a fight every day, so don't be ignorant of his devices. If Satan distracts the saints from their purpose, then he has successfully gotten you where he desires. This is why it is necessary that the saints guard their hearts and ground them in the word of God. Your fight is NOT for popularity, possession, or power; it is to stay the course of faith.

DON'T BE BLINDSIDED BY THE ODDS AGAINST YOU

Nehemiah, a cupbearer to the king Artaxerxes, heard from some men of Judah that the walls of Jerusalem were broken down and that the remnants of Judah were in despair. The men of Judah told him, "Those who survived the exile were in great trouble and disgrace, and that the wall of Jerusalem was broken down and its gates have been burnt with fire" (Nehemiah 1:3). Nehemiah wept for several days fasted and repented for Jerusalem. The city of Jerusalem represented national pride to all Jews. Having its walls ruined and everything within destroyed, its temple, the royal palace, and every vital structure was distressing news to the Jews.

Like Nehemiah, you can attest to having something or someone dear to you destroyed. To make matters worse, all attempts at restoration had failed before. Ezra and the Jews had attempted to rebuild the walls years earlier, but after the protest of Rehum and Shimshai, the king ordered the Jews to desist (Read Ezra 4:7-23). Any mobilization of the Jews to rebuild the walls was met with hostility.

Being the king's cupbearer, Nehemiah earned the King's trust and was subsequently appointed governor over Judah, who permitted him to rebuild the temple walls. However, Nehemiah's request being granted by the king was met with opposition, as the enemies of the children of God will not stand idly by and let them flourish. Just as Rehum and Shimshai opposed the rebuilding of the wall in the days of Ezra, so did Sanballat and Tobiah against Nehemiah.

When the opposing factions heard that Nehemiah and the Jews were rebuilding the wall, they became angry and ridiculed the people of God, saying, what are those feeble Jews doing? Will they restore their wall? Will they offer sacrifices? Will they finish in a day? Can they bring the stones back to life from the heaps of rubble? Even if a fox climbs up on the wall they are building, it will break down! How many times have you been ridiculed for your cause? How many times have you stalled the process, too embarrassed to continue because of the enemies' harassment? This is not new news; Satan will always seek to oppose the children of God, but rest assured that his hostility towards the saints is an attestation of his fear of the saints. Sanballat and Tobiah's intimidation tactics were a sign of their weakness. The trying of the saints' faith worketh patience, so let patience have her perfect work in you. If Nehemiah had allowed Sanballat and Tobiah to bully him, the work would not have been completed.

So do not pay attention to distraction; continue with the work, be determined, remain faithful, and declare like Nehemiah did, "I'm doing great work, and I cannot come down." – THERE IS A CAUSE!

REASON FOR CHASTENING

Too many believers see chastening as a negative occurrence. Chastening can be defined as discipline; however, this is good discipline. The author of Hebrews states that 'if you endure chastening, God deals with you as sons, for what son is he whom the Father chasteneth not?' (Hebrews 12:7-9). Solomon concurs that saint 'should not despise the chastening of the Lord, and we should not be weary of His correction.' (Proverbs 3:11). Like grapes that produce wine when applying pressure. Have you ever wondered why the

Lord allows struggle in your life? Well, like grapes, He is squeezing you into purpose.

Nobody likes being squeezed, but you are His child if the Lord doesn't squeeze you, whom the Father disciplines belong to Him.

In one of my all-time favourite sermons, Bishop Noel Jones shared a story that captivates the concept. He said one day, he was in the gym, and a man who was there took off his shirt, and he noticed that the man had a massive cut from his chest area down to his navel. When he inquired about what had happened, he was told by the man that he had open heart surgery. Jones then proceeded to note a comparison between a man lying in the morgue with a two-inch cut below his chest and the man. On one hand, a man died from a two-inch cut, and the other is alive from an eighteen-inch cut. Jones continued by stating that there are different cuts – some are to kill, others are to save lives. Do you think the Almighty is cutting you too deep and long? Just know that it is not a bad cut once you are His. Just consider that the Lord is performing open heart surgery on you.

I reassure you, "No discipline seems pleasant at the time, but painful. Later on, however, it produces a harvest of righteousness and peace for those who have been trained by it." (Hebrews 12:11). God disciplines His children by adding pressure, which produces righteousness. There is a cause.

Not seeing the good results from your efforts right away does not mean it isn't apparent. So don't let discouragement over an apparent lack of results keep you from working. Instead, do the good that you have an opportunity to do, knowing that, in the end, all things are working for your good – there is a cause.

WISDOM NUGGETS AND EXPRESSIONS

Joseph's father did not give him a regular coat, but one that was special and stood out (multi-coloured). His brothers hated him for it. It shows that some people will hate you for what the Father put on you. Why? Because

you wear it well and it makes you stand out.

The failure to approach anything with an excellence of mind and spirit is already a failure to win.

Moses had a rod in his hand, David had a sling in his hand, Joshua had a sword in his hand, and Samson had an ass' jawbone. It is important to note that what you need, God has already placed it in your hands. However, it is not what you carried in hand but who carried you in (HIS) hand that matters most. So, while you are carrying something of worth in your hands, be pleased to know you are something of worth in HIS hands.

Saul tried to kill David, who was anointed for the role so that he could fit Jonathan in it.

Quit trying to kill the anointed to fit another in it. David's brothers fit the "kingly" physique but weren't anointed for the role. Don't fit them there if they're not anointed for it.

Are you anointed for it, or were you fitted in it? Don't just be fit in the role, be anointed for it. The pit was empty until they put Joseph in it. Sometimes, God will put you in an empty situation for you to fill it. So, quit complaining about **IT** and ask God, what is my assignment in **IT**?

Be mindful that on the road to purpose, not everyone in the passenger seat is there to accompany you to your destination – their goal is to distract you from it.

So, pull over and let them off at the side of the road. If you don't see us riding together anymore, you know why.

The vessel was marred in the hands of the potter, not the hands of the potter marred the vessel. Quit blaming God (The Potter) for your mess and learn to submit while still in His hand.

The consecration could not have started and finished without David's presence because he was the person of interest, though not initially invited. They blocked him, not knowing they were blocking their next king. They have no idea how valuable you are, or they would not have blocked you!

"And the women answered one another as they played, and said, 'Saul hath slain his thousands, and David his ten thousand'" (1 Samuel 18:7).

You don't need to validate to the crowd who you are and the weight you carry – they will see it on you and admit it among themselves! Maybe you are gifted, but have you been divinely designated? Being gifted or special is no excuse for breaching protocol and timing. David, though consecrated, knew his timing – he went back to tend to his father's sheep.

Elisha was given the mantle but still followed and served Elijah, who placed it on him – he needed to know and grow more. Therefore, don't allow your giftedNESS to blind you to Biblical procedures, or else you will end up becoming a giftedness

Mephibosheth was lame from the waist down, but at the King's table, everyone was his equal from the waist up. When the King is done preparing a table for you, even those who had been looking down on you will now have to be looking at you! Remember, the king will make you known.

They only knew about you after you killed a giant. But before that, you had killed a lion and a bear that no one knew about. That's why they think you are an overnight success. Your private encounters will someday reap public acknowledgment. Lazarus was raised before the same people that buried him. Not everyone present showed up to comfort; others came to ensure that he was dead. Be on the alert; marauders are impersonating mourners!

"And the elders of Israel came to Samuel and said, 'Now make us a king to judge us like all the nations.'" The elders perhaps felt that being different (not having a king) from the other nations made them strange. However, the elders failed to see that such differences made them stand out. Sadly, they gave away their uniqueness just to be ordinary. If you have to change who you are to fit in with the crowd, perhaps they were never your crowd in the first place. Be the standout, not the sellout!

Sometimes, God will put you in a hostile environment for you to own it. Daniel was cast in the lion's den, but it became Daniel's den when he got there.

WHAT YOU NEED TO KNOW ABOUT YOUR LEADERS

Those who live to preach the gospel are often relentlessly perplexed to live the gospel they preach. "To whom much is given, much is required" (Luke 12:48). When said in the reverse, to whom much is required has been given. Isn't it funny how some people will point out the requirements but fail to recognize that much is given to the shoulders of the individual to carry? Demand expectations, but at the same time, be sensitive.

While your leaders are called to many, please remember they are just one person. They can't carry out and achieve all the people's demands simultaneously – they are not omnipresent. Please consider that while you glean from your leaders, they need refilling, too. Don't be so selfish! Some of them will not tell you this. Many leaders are the most vulnerable and susceptible after they have finished ministering.

As great as Moses was, there came a time when he had to rely on the strength of others to lift his hands. The beautiful thing is he never had to ask for it – the others saw the necessity. Don't take the greatness of your leaders for granted; they need your strength too.

"And Moses cried unto the Lord, saying, what shall I do unto this people? They are almost ready to stone me." Ungratefulness is confirmed when the ones you nurtured/delivered/loved/empowered/entrusted/encouraged "are ready to stone" you.

THE PRICE OF BEING ANOINTED IS COSTLY. DO YOU STILL WANT IT?

Many people have been taught by the church how to achieve rather than endure. Therefore, they are bewildered when faced with afflictions. You can't successfully achieve if you unsuccessfully endure.

David was not chosen because his brothers were rejected. On the contrary, his brothers were rejected because he was the chosen.

LESSONS ABOUT THE CROWD

Never underestimate who is left back in your crowd – even if they are misfits.

The 300 men that Gideon was left with weren't the best fit (they lapped the water like dogs), yet they were God's fit to take out the Midianites (enemies).

Sometimes, it is better to be released from the crowd than to be adjoined to the crowd. God released Gideon from his crowd.

Some people you must let go. Don't try to hold them back when you let them go – your victory depends on it! The Lord instructed Gideon to let the men go.

Some assignments have to be accomplished without the crowd, lest they say they were the ones that made you.

The Lord told Gideon that he would smite the Midianites as one man.

A decrease in the crowd's volume is **NOT** necessarily a decrease in the crowd's value.

Gideon's army of 300 men was more valuable than 32,000 men.

Only some people in your crowd genuinely want to be there with you. Two-thirds of Gideon's crowd never wanted to be there with him.

Don't use "Judge not, that ye be not judged" to resist correction for wrongdoing – It is no excuse for hypocrisy!

How ironic that you (hypocrites) quote this verse in your rebuttals by using the same to call out "judgment" on others, not knowing that it is speaking about your kind.

Why did Jesus rebuke the wind but only speak to the sea (waves)? Because the wind was what caused the sea's effects. Therefore, Jesus confronted the source of the problem.

On that note, don't expect to be set free from the waves (effect) until you first deliver from the wind (cause). You keep getting the same results because you have been going about it wrong.

SWEETNESS

– will you break God's rule/law just to have it?

Samson ate honey taken from a lion's carcass and gave it to his parents also but did not tell them how he obtained it.

Therefore, be wary of the 'sweet thing' you receive from people - where it is retrieved may be deadly.

On this journey of faith, I have come to the awareness that some mighty and gifted individuals are in Christendom. However, their lust for sweet things has corrupted them and they have blatantly disregarded God's instructions/commands just to acquire the forbidden honey.

"And when the Lord saw that Leah was hated, He opened her womb." Whoever this is for, I just want you to know that God sees your haters and will silence them by giving you an opening! "The blessing of the despised"

God has given us the authority to cast out devils – not to interview them.

MOVING ON

There will come moments in your life where moving on is necessary for your spiritual maturity, progress, success, and stability. Therefore, don't halt the process because "I am stuck." If you have to lower your standards or change who you are to be in their crowd, then they were never your real crowd in the first place.

MOVE ON!

OMAR WEDDERBURN

SCRIPTURES FOR CONSIDERATION

(Matthew 5:48).

En route to purpose, be careful of hitchhikers. Some will pretend to be stranded, but they are actual robbers. MOVE ON!

(Romans 16:17).
They are always silent in your presence but celebrate when you are absent. **MOVE ON!**

(Genesis 37:24-25).

They know you are a whale but keep you in a pond to swim. Can you see their ill intent? **MOVE ON!**

(Romans 4:10, 1 John 2:9).
You will make mistakes and experience disappointments, but it will be worse if you haven't learned any lessons from them. Quit complaining! **MOVE ON!**

(Philippians 3:13, 1 Corinthians 10:11).

Stop knocking on doors that have been shut in your face; you are not invited in! **MOVE ON!**

(Matthew 10:14).

Don't stoop low just to roll high. Be the standout, not the sellout. **MOVE ON!**

(1 Timothy 3:3).

Don't be lured by the devil's treat set before you – God's is always better. Roll your eyes and **MOVE ON!**

(James 1:14-17).
Know when to walk away! If you think you are leaving behind a good thing, wait until God leads you to a better thing. **MOVE ON!**

(Ecclesiastes 7:8, Romans 8:18).

Embrace the reality that some things/people come with expiration. **MOVE ON!**

(Acts 13:2).

Don't lose another night's sleep... You did your best. **MOVE ON!**

(Acts 7:51)

Saul got tormented after David was anointed. Some people will lose their minds about what God will put on you! They can't celebrate with you because they hate what is upon you.

ABOUT AUTHOR

Bishop O'mar Wedderburn hails from the island of Jamaica. He began his walk with the Lord at 16 and was immediately thrust into ministry, serving in the offices of Deacon, Evangelist, and Pastor in 2004. In 2016, He was consecrated to the office of Bishop.

Bishop Wedderburn is a graduate of the Jamaica Theological Seminary. He holds an Associate in Leadership and Ministry, and a Bachelor of Arts in Theology.

He is the author of two books: 'Living on The Edge of a Breakthrough' and Blossoming Through Life's Challenges.

Bishop Wedderburn is considered a prolific speaker, regarded by his peers and contemporaries as an excellent teacher who preaches - delivering the Word of God in a real, relevant, and relatable style.

He is passionate about kingdom networks, youth empowerment, counselling, teaching, discipleship & leadership training.

He fulfils these passions by conducting seminars, workshops, and conferences locally and internationally.

Bishop Wedderburn resides with his darling wife, Kadian, and their children in the UK.

Bishop Wedderburn is obedient to his calling. He is always abundant in the work of the Lord, knowing well that his labour in the Lord is not vain.

OTHER BOOKS BY THE AUTHOR

www.ingramcontent.com/pod-product-compliance
Lightning Source LLC
Chambersburg PA
CBHW070500100426
42743CB00010B/1696